NORTH SOMERSET COAST IN WATERCOLOURS

Sand Bay to the Hotwells lock

Rosie and Howard Smith

The Garret Press

First published in the United Kingdom in November 2005.

The Garret Press, 6 Stafford Place, Weston-super-Mare, Somerset, BS23 2QZ.

British Library Cataloguing in Publication Data.

A catalogue record for this book is available from the British Library.

ISBN

0-9541546-4-9 (paperback)

0-9541546-5-7 (hardback)

Cover illustration: Lighthouse, Black Nore Point, winter.

Design: Colin Baker.

Type: 12 pt. Perpetua.

Printed in Great Britain by: R. Booth Limited, Antron Hill, Mabe, Penryn, Cornwall, TR10 9HH.

ACKNOWLEDGEMENTS

Our thanks to Laura and Allan Hoyano, Kathie Barnes, Catherine Preston, Samuel Smith and Paul Smith for advising on the text. Without them there would have been far too many commas and semicolons. Thanks also to David Brown for his support and to our remarkable designer Colin Baker who has, once again, managed to fit the words to the paintings with graceful effect. We feel the result matches the previous two *in Watercolours* books.

So many people have helped during the two years it took to create this book, but we are especially grateful to: Dave Priddle, Stan and Joan Rendell, Chris Crook, Pat Martin, John Barrett and Brian Austin and, of course, the staff of the local history section of Weston Library. David Nisbet of *Sterling Books* in Weston-super-Mare has been a huge help in obtaining fascinating local material, as has Chris Richards of North Somerset Museum. Discussing various historical aspects with Chris has been a great pleasure - his enthusiasm is so infectious!

We received much kindness and support from Linda Jenkins of Wick St. Lawrence, Franky and Roland Griffin of Kingston Seymour, Jane Lilly of Clevedon, Sandy Tebbutt of Portishead, John Rich of Pill and Reg Coombs of Worle. We hope they don't mind their names popping up in the text.

It was good fun navigating the River Banwell with Paul Cossham in his North American canoe. Andy and Sue Walker's yacht Goldenmean doesn't feature in quite the same way as in the West Somerset book. But we did sail down the coast from Portishead several times, and on one occasion the Weston lifeboat drew up alongside and asked if they could practice rescuing us!

The book was only slowly coming together during the summer of 2005. So, no thanks to the England and Australia Cricket Teams who made the nail-biting Ashes series such an impossible and unbearable distraction.

This book is dedicated to our brothers
Paul, John and George.

INTRODUCTION

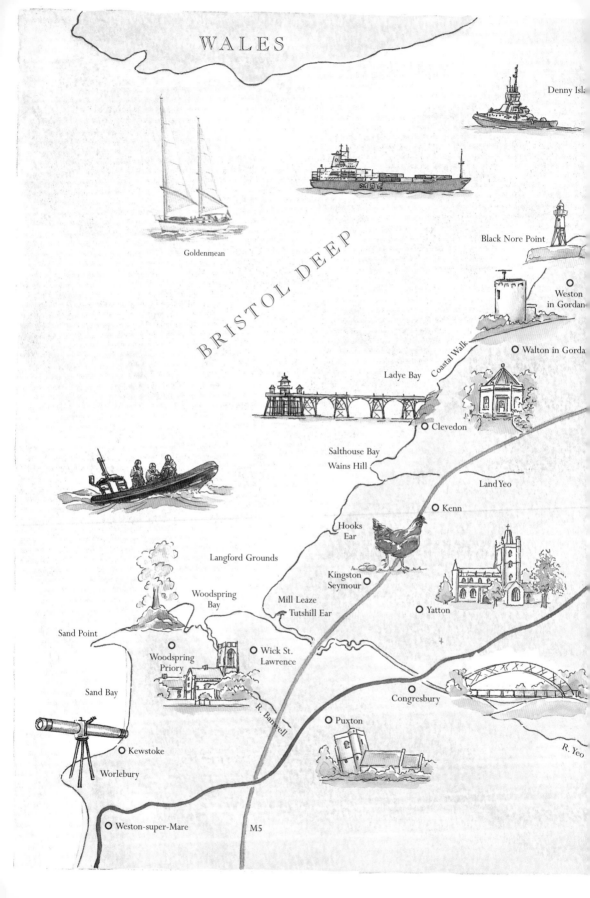

WALES

Denny Isla

Goldenmean

Black Nore Point

BRISTOL DEEP

Weston
in Gordan

Walton in Gorda

Coastal Walk

Ladye Bay

Clevedon

Salthouse Bay
Wains Hill

Land Yeo

Kenn

Hooks
Ear

Langford Grounds

Kingston
Seymour

Yatton

Woodspring
Bay

Mill Leaze
Tutshill Ear

Sand Point

Woodspring
Priory

Wick St.
Lawrence

Congresbury

R. Banwell

Puxton

R. Yeo

Sand Bay

Kewstoke

Worlebury

Weston-super-Mare

M5

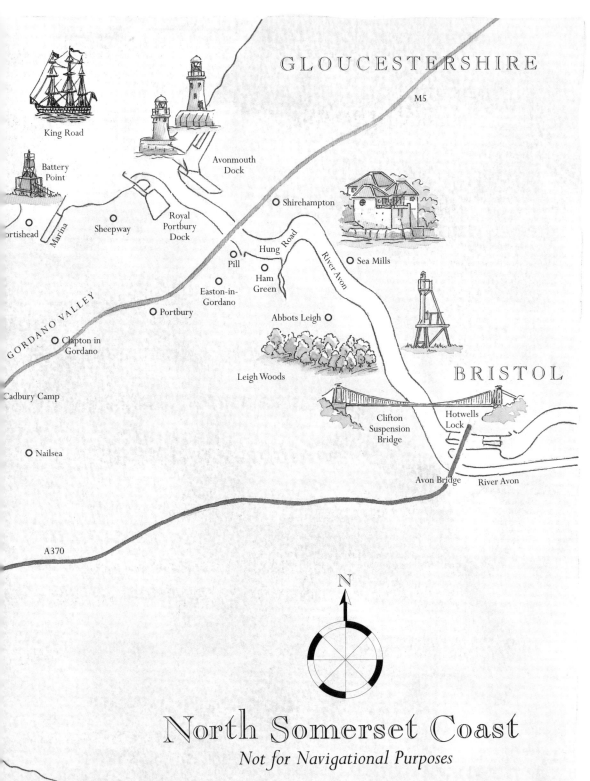

GLOUCESTERSHIRE

M5

King Road

Battery
Point

Avonmouth
Dock

Shirehampton

Marina

Portishead

Sheepway

Royal
Portbury
Dock

Hung Road

Pill

River Avon

Sea Mills

Ham
Green

Easton-in-
Gordano

GORDANO VALLEY

Portbury

Abbots Leigh

Clapton in
Gordano

Leigh Woods

BRISTOL

Cadbury Camp

Nailsea

Clifton
Suspension
Bridge

Hotwells
Lock

Avon Bridge

River Avon

A370

N

North Somerset Coast

Not for Navigational Purposes

INTRODUCTION

The Headlands (circa 1951)

This is the last of three 'In Watercolours' books about the Somerset coast. The story began with 'Weston-super-Mare in watercolours'; an attempt to redress the perception of our home-town. To our surprise and delight, Weston took the book to its heart and so we continued south and west from Weston with West Somerset Coast in watercolours - a journey from Brean Down to the Somerset/Devon border, a mile or two beyond Porlock.

Now we complete the trilogy by moving north-east of Weston, where the Somerset coast describes the county border, taking in: Sand Bay and Sand Point, the pebbled bays of Middle Hope and St. Thomas's Head, Kingston Seymour's marshy levels and on through the seaside towns of Clevedon and Portishead. Somerset's boundary then moves south-east; inland along the south bank of the River Avon, to the old Bristol Channel pilots' harbour of Pill. A mile or so further on, having passed beneath the steepling towers of Brunel's Suspension Bridge, Somerset gives up the river to the City of Bristol and the Floating Harbour of the old port.

Wooded Worlebury Hill shapes the northern boundary to the seaside town of Weston-super-Mare. From the hill's blunt, western promontory, the woods extend eastwards for just over a mile, until the trees meet the residential enclave of Worlebury Park. Thereon, the mix of wood and scrub continues around the hill, its northern and southern slopes interrupted here and there, by roads and abandoned quarries. In its eastern third, the trees encircle Worlebury golf course to close with the exclamation-mark of the white Observatory tower.

My family moved up to Worlebury in 1950, leaving a garden (ie. a basement with tom-cats) flat on the hillside in the Victorian town. Dad had bought a building plot which was cleared with a Second World War landing craft. Roads were unmade, and much of the land between Worlebury Park and the golf course was filled by market gardens that provided Weston with most of its fruit and veg.

The bottom of our road (eventually to be called Furze Road) looked north - out over Sand Bay and the sea. Through a gap in a hawthorn hedge, marked by a gas streetlight, my sister, brothers and I (and a few others) allowed ourselves into a land we called 'the headlands'. Here, a multitude of rabbits kept the grass short, springy and comfortable to sprawl on; a backcloth to a scatter of mole and ant-hills, and clumps of hawthorn and bramble. But the best things about this special place were the clefts and crannies on the escarpment below the grassy hilltop. From here, on the north side of the hill overlooking Kewstoke, we could watch out over Sand Bay and the Channel. I had a telescope (an ex-naval gunsight bought from Headquarter and General Supplies Ltd) which weighed a ton, and for which I fashioned a tripod from Meccano and three stair-rods. The tripod was a trifle short; so we had to squat or lie down to get to the eyepiece, but through its misty glass we could investigate the lightship five miles off St. Thomas's Head or the lighthouse on Flat Holm (Steep Holm was hidden by the hill, but we knew it was there); the steelworks along the Welsh coast (whose Bessemer converters would flame the night sky); Campbell steamers plying between the Old Pier at Birnbeck and Newport or Penarth; and the first caravans gathering in the fields below.

Along 'our' north Somerset coast, the scene was ever-changing. With spring tides, the gunmetal sea would slip away beyond Sand Point to reveal the sand banks of the Langford Grounds between Weston and Clevedon. Further out, patches of the English Grounds would show themselves, forming the eastern boundary of the shipping channel known, timber-shiveringly, as the Bristol Deep. We took the tidal arrival and departure for granted, only learning years later, with amazement, that after the Bay of Fundy in East Canada, it was the second largest rise and fall on the planet (some say it's actually the third, but that would spoil the amazement).

Living on Worlebury, we were ever aware of our corner of the Severn Sea. The same wind inciting white horses in the Channel rattled the windows at home and tore branches from the elms and ash trees in our garden. Through early summer, each evening sun would move a little further along the horizon to set in the north-west beyond the Welsh Hills. Most times, as it left the sky, it trailed clouds of dazzling, fiery brilliance. In winter, cold, clear days with bright, low sunlight made the coastline stand out with startling definition. But winter could fill the Bristol Channel with sea-fog; grey-dark by day, impenetrable by night. Then, the siren foghorns would wail out from Flat Holm; great, gut-wrenching roars you heard through your skin rather than your ears - I can still feel the great sound ending with its desperate, collapsing, 'wumff'...

And it is Worlebury where this book begins.

Chapter One

Monks Hill

From Worlebury's ridge above Kewstoke village, there were once many ways
of getting down to the shoreline, mostly by old footpaths now long fallen into disuse.
But immediately below what a bevy of 1950's children called *'the headlands'* (now
occupied by bungalows along Cliff Road) there was an easy descent to the fields
alongside the Kewstoke Road - a road which soon divides to take us either along the
Toll Road to Weston-super-Mare or, by a curving descent, into Sand Bay. For the rest
of Worlebury, the more usual route to and from Kewstoke was by way of Monks Hill -
the most fearsome gradient in the district. The surprise right-angle bend at its steepest
point stalled innumerable cars (it still does!!), to be followed, in those presynchromesh

days, by a desperate scraunching struggle for first gear.[1] At the point where Monks Hill turns and plunges downwards there once stood 'The Monks Rest Tea Gardens', created and watched over by the Overy family. As well as fantastic views over Kewstoke and the bay, the cafe had a lovely, rickety old-worldliness of benches, wobbly tables and very bad telescopes. The strawberries and cream were pretty good though.

A much older way down the hill still exists. Monks Steps (known to the Victorians as 'The Pass of St. Kew') runs from Woodspring Avenue, opposite St. Paul's School, to intersect half way down with Monks Hill[2] (See Special Page on Monks Steps). Crossing the road and climbing over and down the facing stone wall, the Steps continue through a woodland garden, to emerge opposite Kewstoke's St. Paul's Church. I remember a narrower Monks Steps running down a bare ravine with a scree of limestone at its lower end. Today, the ravine has filled with trees to become a combe and the Steps have been excavated to reveal an impressive, wide stone stairway.

At its bottom end, Monks Hill crash-lands onto the Kewstoke Road; a highway which keeps itself busy running all the way around the northern semicircle of Worlebury Hill - from Worle village, through Kewstoke and along the toll road to Birnbeck above the Old Pier in Weston.[3] Opposite the T-junction stands the small church-hall where my sister and younger brothers once attended Sunday School. The old stone porch they entered by has gone; only its outline in the mortar remains. It opened directly on to the road and inevitably, perhaps, the entrance was moved - to its east wall near the church gate.[4] But why that awful flat roof?

[1] The road sign says 1:4, but it's definitely steeper than that in places. In the days before global-warming, snow was a frequent visitor up on Worlebury, and it only needed a dash of the stuff to render Monks Hill impassable. Defeated cars slid backwards down the slope and often ended up lashed to one of the hill's gas-lamps - once, rather optimistically I thought, with someone's tie!

[2] In cutting the road during the mid-19th century, part of the lower steps was lost.

[3] In my doctoring days, a house-call to Kewstoke Road could mean Weston, Worle, Kewstoke or anywhere in-between. A problem at 3 o'clock in the morning.

[4] The church hall was once Kewstoke's poorhouse and became the village school in the 1840s. The school proper now occupies a handsome Edwardian building, constructed against the hillside, close to the church.

From the porch, St. Paul's Church

From the road, the land falls gently away such that the stepped path from the gate invites you to the church. St. Paul's has Norman origins (12th century) - confirmed by a beautiful, arched stone doorway, hidden away inside the south porch - but had substantial rebuilds during the 15th and 19th centuries.[5] Only a few years ago, an aged sycamore sheltered the comings and goings along the church path. But, despite the decline and loss of the old tree, the surrounding churchyard[6] remains a consoling and reflective place. Over the wall to the west, and completing the picture, stands the good-looking Georgian rectory which now serves as a guest-house.

Crooks Lane, descending north and then west behind the church, has many of the village's oldest cottages and farmhouses (17th & 18th century). They cluster in the protective lee of the hill although, being in Worlebury's shadow, they are hard pressed for sunshine during the winter months. To the rear of the New Inn is the terrace of Victory Cottages, built in 1759, and so named in celebration of General Wolfe's defeat of the French in Quebec. At the lower end of the terrace, an eccentric village pump stands to attention within its privately paved recess. To me, it looks as though it was fashioned from a drain pipe. Sadly, with its pump-arm locked firmly to its side, it pumps no more. Close by, the scene, looking back up the hill, low cotts against the lowering tower of St. Paul's and the wooded hillside, encapsulates the character of the village. It's the stuff of postcards!

[5] In 1849, repairs to the north wall revealed a small wooden cup in an 18 inch stone cavity. The cup appeared to be stained with blood. This led to the speculation that it was a reliquary of Thomas a Beckett (murdered in Canterbury Cathedral in 1170) and moved from Woodspring Priory at the time of the Dissolution of the Monasteries.

[6] Local historian Sue Ryall tells the story of George Prescott who 'dug a few graves in his spare time'. He helped with a grave behind the church but the ground was very stony. "So a man came from Butt's Quarry with some explosive to make the hole bigger!" The Rector's wife expressed the opinion that she would prefer to be buried somewhere a bit less rocky.

Something on a quite different scale arrived in 1933, when the Birmingham Hospital Saturday Fund built the Kewstoke Convalescent Home. Styled in the manner of a Pharaonic Grand Hotel, parading on the Promenade des Anglais in Nice, it succeeds, somehow, in keeping largely out of sight - despite being a dazzle of white paint.[7] Whenever I was called to see patients there, the quality of the home's internal decor always amazed me - a wonderful High Deco style of tall windows, marbled walls, wooden floors, dramatic staircases and French windows opening onto a colonnaded verandah. From two raised terraces, a wide pavement swept down to the seashore across expansive lawns. A most extraordinary convalescent home! At its height, there were over 100 recuperating patients here - originally women only - cared for by Matron and her Nursing Team, a Head Gardener and 8 gardeners, kitchen and room staff, and even a First Engineer! But now the need for charitable convalescence appears to have come to an end. Other BHSF institutions have closed in Weston and the Kewstoke Home is the last to go. Hopefully, the building and its grounds will continue as an integrated estate and its wide, open aspect preserved.

[7]*During the war, the Home was swiftly converted into a military hospital and many servicemen came here to recover after the evacuation of Dunkirk. Its snowy whiteness made it something of a bombing target and a useful landmark for German bombers. So it was painted with army camouflage. The lawns were dug up to grow vegetables. I 'm told the Home is built entirely of engineering bricks;"All the walls are harder than granite. When they were installing en-suite bathrooms a while back, they were going through drill bits like nobody's business!" I suspect a bomb or two would have made little impression either.*

Coastline below Kewstoke Toll Road

In 1848 John Hugh Smyth-Pigott, Lord of the Manor, decided on a marine drive to embellish the wooded estate he had planted on Worlebury Hill. He elected to follow the track of an ancient pathway called Black Rock Path[8], which threaded its way, from Kewstoke into Weston, above the cliffs of the hill's northern shoreline. At either end of the road he built a gatehouse - a handsome villa at the Weston end and in Kewstoke, a more rustic, Gothic cottage affair - but with castellations.[9] He succeeded in creating an enchanting road. Coming from Weston, you catch elusive glimpses of Sand Bay and Sand Point between the trees which can then suddenly open out to show the full breadth of the shoreline. Travelling from Kewstoke, the mood is quite different; the side of the hill proceeds ahead of you in a series of rocky coves, with Birnbeck and its dark pier visible in startling breaks above the cliffs.

Although franchises come and go, the road continues to pay its way and is known to all in the area as 'The Toll Road' - but bicycles and pedestrians (because this was always a public right of way) are free. And that's the best way to enjoy it.

[8]*Black Rock Path led to the 'Mulpit Stone' near the shore at Sand Bay - the boundary marker to the manor of Weston-super-Mare. Chris Richards of North Somerset Museum has been unable to locate it. The stone is probably buried under flood defence work to the shoreline.*

[9]*Both these buildings have been lost. I watched the small cottage slowly fall to bits over the years. But the Weston gatehouse, in an act of inexplicable civic vandalism, was demolished in 1967 - the two houses now occupying its site belong more to a 1970's housing estate. A sister building to the gothic lodge still stands, at the entrance to the woods, on Worlebury Hill Road.*

Monks Steps

The Pass of St. Kew

Originally known as 'The Pass of St Kew' (it appears to have changed its name in the late 19th century), Monks Steps were probably a medieval church-path from the hamlet of Milton, on the south side of the hill, to its parish church of St Paul in Kewstoke. St Kew was a female saint whose hermitage was thought to be at the top of the Steps. Her name goes back to the Dark Ages (5th - 9th centuries) and is linked to the very beginnings of Christianity in the West Country. However; she's something of a rarity; her name occurring in only a few other places - one being St Kew in Cornwall where she crops up along with her brother St Docco. Interestingly, it's her scarcity that gives her association with Kewstoke and the young church added validity. In addition to this, as well as giving her name to the first part of Kewstoke, the 'stoke' component is often a place-name for a religious settlement. (There are other theories: that the name arises from the Celtic 'Kewch' - a boat, so it's 'a place of boats' or; the Norman 'chiw' - a ridge, so it's 'a village on the ridge'. Take your pick.)

The dimensions of St Paul's nave suggest Anglo-Saxon origins (pre-1066) and the 'sub-oval' shape of the original churchyard boundary hints at an even earlier Saxon ancestry. All this may mean that Kewstoke is a very early Christian site indeed.

About three quarters of the way up the Steps, on the right hand side, is a deep pit, which resembles the pits found at Worlebury's Iron Age hill-fort, further to the west. Jacksons' 1877 *Visitor's Handbook to Weston-super-Mare* describes "an oblong pit with masonry" and later investigations to have revealed " the remains of a stone structure on a platform". At one time it was claimed that by pressing your ear to the nearby rock-face; "you could hear the sound of rushing water". All this has given rise to the speculation this was an early well-chapel where people were baptised and tributes were left. Such well-chapels are often found at coastal sites, a short distance from their ecclesiastical settlement. However; a late Victorian excavation suggested St Kew's Well had Iron Age origins, so it may well have been a truly ancient cult-site which was taken over by the early Christians.

It became an especially interesting hole in the ground when my cousin, Ralph Jackson, fell into it - he had become detached from the rocks he was climbing above the pit.

See: Somerset Archaeology and Natural History Vol. 147 2004
Early Ecclesiastical Sites in Somerset: Three Case Studies. Michael Calder.

Chapter Two

SAND BAY

Sand Bay looking to Sand Point

Sand Bay's[10] wide beach stretches nearly 2 miles, in a gentle arc, from wooded
Worlebury Hill to the grassy promontory of Sand Point. At low tide, a huge expanse
of sand and mud reveals itself, organised into a succession of bands from the high-water
mark. First come low sand-dunes with barbed sea buckthorn and Marram grass.
Then the strandline; a zone of bleached logs, shattered trees and dried out wrack
seaweeds thrown beyond the high-water mark by the spring tides. Most of the flotsam
and jetsam ends up around here and, to Sand Bay's discomfort, it's where the currents
conspire to dump a lot of the Bristol Channel's
junk. But the fermenting heaps of
seaweed are a haven for sandhoppers
(sort of leaping shrimps) which jump
around like party-poppers when
disturbed by an inquisitive boot.
Next comes a wide area of hard,
yellow sand (good for walking,
horse-riding - and cricket!) edged
by a band of tellin shells that crunch
and crackle underfoot. This is
followed by a region of wet sand
inhabited by lugworms, their piled-up
casts of coiled sand betraying them
to fishermen who dig them up for bait.

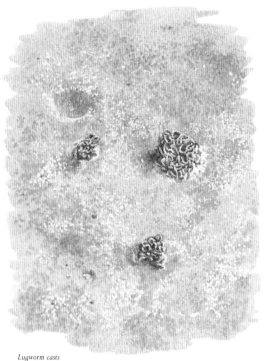

Lugworm casts

Just beyond the lugworms lie traps
for the unwary; places where mud lurks
beneath a thin covering of sand looking much like the firm stuff you've just strolled
over. Suddenly, the sandy crust gives way and your shoes are enveloped by Severn
Estuary silt (mud) - better to be here in bare feet when the sensation can be curiously
pleasant, though it may lurk for days between your toes.

[10]*In the early 1800s, Sand Bay's seashore was described as having a seaward ridge between Worlebury
and Sand Point know as 'The Old Strand' and the bay consisted
of a wide sweep of uninterrupted, fine sand.*

Despite years of living with the peril of Worle 'coming round the corner', Kewstoke remains a rural community and still feels like a real village. Up until the last war, 'the seaside' played a small, though important, part in the local economy. Cafes and general stores came and went along the bay - constantly, it seemed, reinventing themselves[11]. Bungalows and chalets, interspersed with a few caravan parks, inched their way along Beach Road. Around about 1938, a holiday camp arrived, to be taken over and expanded by Fred Pontin in 1947. For the first time, holiday makers began to arrive in fair numbers on Sand Bay beach. In 1999 Pontin's sold up and the camp became 'Sand Bay Holiday Village'.

Even with the sea on its doorstep, fishing appears, historically, to have played a relatively small role in Kewstoke village life - presumably because of better anchorage at Weston.[12] Where The Commodore Hotel now stands, at the south end of the bay under Worlebury Hill, there was once a row of fishermen's cottages. They were absorbed into the hotel, as it grew around them, in the 1960s. On Sand Point and Middle Hope, shrimp fishing was active into the 1950s, and boys of the village would gather winkles from the rocks to sell in the local pubs. Along Birnbeck's stony causeway and at Middle Hope, nets were strung up on poles to snare fish with the retreating tide. There's some speculation the sea once lapped below the bluff St.Paul's Church stands on, and the Pass of St. Kew (Monks Steps) was a defensible passage from the old landing ground. Who knows?

[11] *My father, in a white heat of entrepreneurial gusto, hired out a surplus penny weighing machine from his pharmacy to one of the beach shops. But the coin-slot kept blocking up with sand and he never took much more than £2 in a season.*

[12] *However; seafarers were passing through. According to F.A. Knight, the parish register records poor relief provision in 1695 and 1702 - "given to 24 seamen which had been taken by ye French - 2 shillings" and - " gave unto 7 poor ship carpenters that had their bones broken in Bristol - 1 shilling". Knight notes that this "was not an excessive sum"!*

Sand Bay and its adjoining low lying fields constitute part of the Northmarsh[13] flood plain. Over the centuries, whenever tide, wind and rainfall have conspired, the sea has invaded the land with dangerous regularity. The most recent was not that long ago the Great Storm of December 1981 - when many of the houses and businesses fronting the shoreline suffered very badly. From time to time even tornados may make a call![14]

Way back, in 1606, sea defences along the entire Somerset coastline were breached, with flood waters reaching as far inland as Glastonbury. The small, farming hamlets of Collum and Culm,[15] some 2 km. inland from Sand Bay, occupy a slight rise in the land which explains why they are so placed - those few extra metres must have afforded them some protection whenever the sea broke through.[16]

[13]The Northmarsh (also known as the North Somerset Levels), separated from the Somerset Levels by the Mendips, extends along the coast from Uphill in the south to Clevedon in the north.
Inland, it takes in the low land west of Locking, Banwell, Congresbury, Yatton and Tickenham.

[14]11th January 2004, a tornado, visible from Sand Bay, lifted a waterspout from the mid-Bristol Channel close to Steep Holm. The sky went very dark, almost black, with spray and thunder. Fortunately, it spun off towards Wales where it petered out - its 114 mph winds could have caused considerable damage.

[15]According to Knight, Collum and Culm are possibly derived from the Norse 'kulum', meaning 'at the mounds', ie. the higher ground the farms stand on.

[16]But not always. Recalling a mid-19th century flood which happened in her childhood, a woman, some 80 years later, recounted - "...and my father opened the back door (at Culm) and a great wave knocked him backwards.
Next morning I came over with my mother to Collum...
Mrs Rattles, she was sweeping out the bottom of the house and all the little children they was sticking their heads out of the bedroom windows..."

Walking that way today, along Elmsley and Foss Lanes, mid-September, the sea seems far away - the high hawthorn hedgerows are laden with scarlet haws, orange-red hips of the dog rose and an abundance of blackberries. All the while, sand martins and their distinctive twittering skitter down the lanes and over the hedges, diving to speed-feed on insects above the rhynes and stubbled fields. Elmsley Lane, which is still mainly a grassy track, must have been the summer way from Kewstoke to Woodspring Priory. Its name holds the memory of a lost landscape; when elm trees stood high along the field boundaries, rough leafed, resisting the salt laden westerlies of the Northmarsh. In the 1970s, Dutch elm disease put paid to these magnificent, high-standing, timber trees; but they live on in the hedgerows, hemmed in with the hawthorn, waiting for the wretched pestilence to pass.[17]

From where they divide; Fosse Lane curves away to Wick St. Lawrence, while Elmsley Lane accompanies the Kewstoke Rhyne towards Woodspring Priory. On this September day, in one rhyne-bound field, hay has been cut and rolled into shredded wheats. Below the coastal rise of Middle Hope and St. Thomas's Head, the monastic barn, farmhouse and Perpendicular tower of the priory are touched by sunlight, and Elmsley Lane climbs the gentle incline towards Collum and Culm. There, it joins the road from Worle, dipping back down the slope towards the priory.

[17]*The English elm throws suckers from its roots, so most trees in a hedgerow will be clones of one another. It is this lack of genetic variation which may partly explain why resistance to Dutch elm disease has failed to emerge. Elms can still achieve a reasonable 'tree-size', but once their trunk circumference exceeds 14 cm the bark-beetle, carrying the malignant Ceratocystis fungus, will be sure to arrive ...*

All the older maps (my relatively recent 1958 Ordnance Survey included) show a hamlet called 'Sand' about midway along the bay, close to where Sand Farm now lies. Presumably this was never more than a collection of agricultural buildings, but it was big enough to donate its name to Sand Bay. There is still a public footpath (Sand Farm Lane) running from the beach. It passes by Sand Farm (which has suffered a 20th century makeover) and across the front-yard of a stud farm, flanked by two concrete towers[18]. The path then presses along a tight corridor between hedges until it breaks cover, crossing fields and rhynes, to eventually meet up with Elmsley Lane. These are old ways, and they are becoming increasingly obscured in the haphazard development along Beach Road.

[18]*These two towers began life as concrete storage silos. They were amongst the first in the land and, I understand, were nearly listed as being of architectural merit. They are not entirely beautiful.*

The topography of the bay has changed a lot since Rosie and I roamed here in the 1950s and 60s. Then, the beach was much lower and there was a substantial sea-wall defending the shoreline at the Worlebury end. The Second World War blockhouse, on the beach just north of Sand Farm, stood quite high among the dunes, whereas now it is half submerged in sand. The 1981 storm underlined the inadequacies of Sand Bay's sea-defences and the economic solution arrived at in 1983 was 'The Sand Bay Beach Renourishment Scheme'[19].

[19]*The renourishment scheme took longer than originally planned - eight months rather than three (1983/84). The dredger pumps proved to be inadequate and storms damaged equipment. Early on, a pontoon broke free and smashed into the pier causeway at Birnbeck, fracturing two of the cast iron supports and damaging five others. For a while, it looked as though the Old Pier was fatally injured, but subsequent repairs were successful. The entire scheme cost over £2 million. Back in 1935, Reg Simmonds and seven fellow workmen laboured for six months at Sand Bay building a mile long, 8 ft high, clay wall. They 'mined' clay from the sea bed and brought it ashore with the help of two horses hired from a local farmer. The workmen were paid 1 shilling (5p) an hour and the entire clay-wall scheme cost £1,000!*

Sand and gravel were dredged from the central area of the Bristol Channel, pumped along huge pipes to be laid out, in heaps, along the shoreline. Mechanical diggers then pushed it into its final position; in some places 12 feet higher than the previous level. So that's why the sea-wall disappeared and the Army blockhouse seemed to sink. Also, at the northern end of the bay, the dune area has broadened into a grassy plateau, much wider than before, and part inhabited by scrub and sea-buckthorn. For some years after the 'renourishment', the bay seemed scruffy and the gravel marked your clothes. Now, the seashore has settled down, the proper sand has returned (mixed with mysterious bits of flint[20]), and the Northmarsh, hopefully, protected for the foreseeable future.

The blockhouse, Sand Bay

[20]*The River Severn is Britain's longest stream, flowing north-east from its source in the central Welsh mountains above Llanidloes to cross the country's border just west of Shrewsbury. It then flows south, west of Birmingham and Worcester to Gloucester from where it broadens into its estuary. On its way, the river and its tributaries pass through many geologies; so the gravel of the Bristol Channel contains a complex mix of rock - including flint.*

At its north end, near Sand Point Farm, Beach Road returns to something like its old form - much as it was before the post-war march of the bungalows. Elder, bramble, willow, grey poplar and hawthorn shroud the road, sand spills out over the tarmac where a second blockhouse stands guard (there's a third in a field close by). The road, seemingly, tunnels its way towards the Point. On the seaward side, the sand of the bay abruptly turns green where an extensive acreage below Sand Point has been invaded by Spartina grass[21]. For as long as I can remember, enormous anxiety has been expressed about the Spartina colonising the entire bay and for years its march did appear inexorable as various attempts to dig it up and poison it to death failed. Nowadays, its progress does seem to have slowed, although some worrying clumps have set up camp in the middle of the bay - like advance parties to an imminent invasion. Sand Point and Bay are listed as Sites of Special Scientific Interest and English Nature, at the time of writing, is against the removal of the Spartina - it considers the grass aids sand-dune stabilisation and encourages wildlife along the strandline.

Spartina 'meadow', Sand Bay

[21] *Spartina grass; either Spartina x townendii, a hybrid of an American grass and European cord grass (and, like many hybrids, it's very vigorous!) or Sp. angelica. It wasn't meant to be in Sand Bay at all. In 1913, a misguided individual planted it to stabilise the shoreline at Wick St Lawrence and Kingston Seymour. In 1932 it was first noticed in Sand Bay and by 1940 it had spread throughout the Severn estuary.*

Opposite Sand Point Farm, a path leads through a thicket of hawthorn and apple trees (which, from their flavour, I took to be Worcesters) down to the beach, where the Spartina grass stretches away like a meadow to Sand Point. Rosie spent much of her childhood here, burrowing through the scrub, making dens and forgetting to go home for lunch. This 'meadow' is true saltmarsh; covered regularly by the tide - as evidenced by clumps of seaweed along its landward edge. About here, a stone sea-wall emerges and runs for 100 yards or so, to the crook of the promontory.

Rosie Smith
'The Sand Bay Years'
1958 - 1968

Rosie's dad, Peter Smith, had a dream of living by the sea. The family often visited Weston, so when the chance of a brand new bungalow on Sand Bay's Beach Road (no. 75) came up, he jumped at it. They brought the nameplate (Mount Carmel) of their house in Horfield, Bristol, with them and Pete screwed it up above the front door. But living right on the coast proved to be a challenge. It was always windy - too windy to ever use the front door. "So everyone went in round the back". Pete struggled with a variety of chimney cowls, in a vain attempt to stop the living room filling with smoke. Rosie's mum, Maud, battling with sand in every cranny, soon found that Sand Bay was really quite isolated.

Continued

It was a long walk to the few shops in Crooks Lane, Kewstoke, and ages by bus into Weston. Milk and newspapers were delivered by horse and cart, fish arrived in a van, with another supplying fruit & veg, once a week. And all the while, Pete was working in Bristol, and brother Paul doing the same journey to school.

But for Rosie, it was eternal summer. Endless sunny days out on the beach and "Mum blowing a whistle for me to come in for meals". Every moment possible was spent in the sand-dunes and undergrowth just where the prom wall stopped, north of 'Sand Bay Stores'.

"We made dens where no-one could find us, with tunnels that would only let children through." Later, summer days brought plenty of seasonal work. "My first job was at the car park at the bottom of Sand Point - before it was taken over by The National Trust. It was run by Mary in an invalid chair. She had a leather bag for the parking fees and she used to collect me on her way to the Point. There was a shed (close to where the loos now are) where she used to have her afternoon nap. When she was asleep I sometimes rode around in her chair. I don't think she knew." Meanwhile, unaware of all this, I was peering down at Sand Bay, from the Worlebury headlands, through my Navy Surplus gunsight.

In those days, Pontin's Holiday Camp had its own riding stables run by the Bliss family. "At the start I drove a pony and trap, but later I took out horses and people on rides along the beach, I was only 12 or 13. Sometimes there were a dozen riders and the horses were huge! It was preposterous!! Mum thought 'it wasn't quite right'. Which was true. But it was great! Another summer holiday, I worked as a chalet maid at Pontin's - mornings and weekends. Tea breaks in the boiler room with the 'senior' chalet maids. Cleaning the rooms while the campers were still in the bathroom or even in bed!"

Eventually Rosie took a step up to work at 'Forte's No.2 Ice Cream Parlor' opposite the Marine Lake in Weston.

Chapter Three

SAND POINT, MIDDLE HOPE
AND ST. THOMAS'S HEAD

Across the bay, Sand Point to Worlebury, late afternoon

Sand Point is a ridge of hard, Carboniferous Limestone[22] rising some 48m above sea level and extending, by just over 1 km, out into the Bristol Channel. The ridge runs back, west-east, for 3 km to overlook the pebbled coves of Middle Hope and the rocky foreland of St. Thomas's Head. Tucked below this protective rise, lie the farm and ecclesiastical buildings of Woodspring Priory. Since 1963, this precious area of coastline has been in the safe keeping of The National Trust.[23]

[22]*Sand Point, Worlebury, Brean Down and much of the Mendip Hills are made up of Carboniferous Limestone, laid down by marine organisms in shallow, tropical seas about 360 million years ago. The stone is dense, weather resistant and varying grey in colour. Up to the 1920s, it was used extensively as building stone in the Weston-super-Mare area.*

[23]*In 1963, Sand Point was donated to The National Trust by Graham Burrough of Bridport. Middle Hope and Woodspring were acquired in 1968.*

From the Trust's comfortable, south facing car-park at the bottom of Sand Point (some get no further than here), there are several ways up onto the higher ground. The most accessible is the easy slope which runs out to sea, along the southern aspect of the promontory (the other routes are more direct and steeper). This sheltered side of the hill has a luxuriant growth of hawthorn, ash, wild clematis, even the occasional apple tree, all meeting to form a canopy over the upper end of the path. For a while here, the sea is hidden by the trees; reduced to a persistent, tireless murmuring. Beyond a five-bar gate, the trees give way to bramble and scrub so you emerge, with a feeling of release, to the southward sweep of Sand Bay and the recurring promontories of Worlebury and Brean Down. Then, it's a short climb to the Point's summit (marked by a concrete 'trig' point) where the full panorama of the Severn Sea opens up, to the north and the south. A short distance further west, the ground is disturbed and scarred by the remains of earthworks, dykes and ditches - the carcass of an Iron Age encampment.[24]

Walking out to sea along the Point, the limestone strata slides to the south, as the escarpment follows an undulating descent to the tip of the promontory. There, the sea snarls in stony shallows - a zone of never-ending turbulence called, benignly, Swallow Rocks. Standing aboard Sand Point feels different from its sibling protrusions; on Worlebury, the woods virtually obscure the sight of the sea and you are limited to either a north or south perspective; Brean Down, though largely clear of trees is a much bigger affair and rises, like Worlebury, to about 100m - twice the height of Sand Point. So, on the Point, the sea surrounds you, and it's like walking a low tightrope slung out above the tide. On the south side, the Spartina grass has advanced well out to sea, cresting longitudinal hillocks in the mud. The tide traces a rippled curve across the bay to Birnbeck, silt and sea merging at a glistening edge.

[24]*A much smaller affair than the Worlebury hill-fort, possibly a defensive position, protecting a landing place in Middle Hope. The 'trig' point itself is sat upon a 'castle batch' or a beacon site. F.A.Knight tells of a map (The Coste of England uppon Severne), from the time of Henry VIII, showing three round towers, each with 2 guns, providing part of Somerset's sea-defences. One tower supposedly stood on Uphill, one at Weston and the third at Woodspring. It seems they were never built, although in 1810, a mound of earth and stones still stood on the promontory - possibly the ruins of a round tower. The present day 'trig' point stands on the remains of a Bronze Age burial mound.*

Crinoid fossils in stone wall, Middle Hope

In summer, it's easy to find a sheltered place. The grass is springy and soft, close cropped by rabbits, cattle and sheep. Rosie and I settle down with our backs to the rocks. Looking north east, across the coastal pasture of Middle Hope, we can make out Clevedon; just visible above the hill-line. The rocks are crusted with golden lichens and the crannies filled by Biting stonecrop.[25] On occasions we've been lucky to see the rare Glanville fritillary butterfly[26] flitting low over the grassy slopes. Sand Point is home to a number of rare plants, but it's safe to mention the White rock rose - probably a deliberate transplant from Brean Down where it grows in unique abundance and flowers in early June. Rock samphire grows freely on the sunny southern cliffs, and although nobody I know pickles its fleshy leaves these days, it's once again becoming a fashionable delicacy. The grassland itself is considered 'richly unimproved' - sustained by animal grazing - which means, that above those same south cliffs, the very rare Somerset hairgrass is able to survive.

[25]*Biting stonecrop. Sedum acre. This plant intrigues me. If you chew on its succulent leaves; it bites back - for, after a few seconds delay, you get a definite peppery chilli heat. It has bright yellow flowers in summer. Apparently, it was planted on roofs to ward off thunderstorms!*

[26]*The Glanville fritillary is reckoned to survive only on the Isle of Wight, but I've definitely seen it on Sand Point - and so has The National Trust. It's a small orange-brown butterfly with dotted orange spots on its hind-wings.*

Across the plateau are stone walls[27] some of which were erected by prisoners captured during the Napoleonic wars. One, demarcating an extended enclosure on the northern side of the promontory, is 2 metres (7 ft) high and solidly intact. Further to the east, the field wall is largely ruinous, serving no purpose other than to look picturesque.

Volcanic outcrop at Swallow Cliff

[27] *The limestone walls are chock-full of crinoid fossils - feathery branched animals (sea-lilies) with long jointed stalks (the bits that got fossilised) by which they attached themselves to the beds of ancient seas. They belong to the Echinoderms; the group of animals that includes starfish and sea urchins. Some rock strata are so full of fossils they are called 'Crinoid limestones'. The detached joints have been called 'St. Cuthbert's Beads'.*

A short distance back from the Point, we make our way down to the most westerly of Middle Hope's four bays to where the pasture shelves, in a relaxed gradient, from the higher ground. These bays are the reason why this area is a Site of Special Scientific Interest, for here, sometime in the aeonian past, submarine volcanic eruptions of lava and ash burst between the strata of the Carboniferous Limestone[28] - one of only three such places in the British Isles. The eruptions might well have been part of the colossal force that tilted and distorted the strata's alignment in the creation of the Mendip Hills - the so-called 'Armorican or Hercynian orogeny'. The limestones themselves are especially rich in fossils and it's easy to find black-grey pebbles filled with white fragments of crinoid stems, corals and shellfish. Give them a lick and they'll come up good as new!

[28] There are 3 sites of Carboniferous volcanic activity at Middle Hope with a lesser one on MoD land at St. Thomas's Head. The volcanic rock is quite different to the over and underlying limestone. Lava, flowing from underwater volcanoes, solidified rapidly into great congealed green/black clumps called 'pillow basalt' - rare in the British Isles. There is also greeny soft stone ('tuff') formed from volcanic ash exploding into the air and settling back on top the laval flow. It is these softer rocks that have eroded leaving deep grooves in the cliff face and also allowing the formation of the coves.

Looking west from the small bay, the tilt of the rock strata forms a low escarpment called Swallow Cliff[29], running a jagged course, to the nib of the Point. Out on the sea-line sits Flat Holm with its lighthouse - its sister river-island, Steep Holm, out of sight from here, down channel. Moving due east along the cliff top, Rosie and I reach a ruined stone building - the remains of a shrimp fishermen's house - built into the shelving hillside above a gully leading down to the sea. It's here the small, sweet, 'Weston' shrimps would be netted offshore and brought to the hut where they would be cleaned and cooked. They would then be carried across the headland to Sand Bay and then to Weston fishmongers and pubs. At times, the harvest would be so bountiful, the market would be overwhelmed and surplus shrimps and fish would be used for pig-swill or fertiliser! In a corner of the shrimp house, a few bricks of the shrimp-boiler still stand and there's a fireplace - with plenty of driftwood to burn; it must have been a cosy, steamy place of a winter's evening.[30]

The shrimp hut, Middle Hope

[29] *Why Swallow Cliff? - it's there on my 1809 Ordnance map. Swallow Rocks and Swallow Bay seem more recent arrivals. Maybe it's because swallows and martins travel up and down the Bristol Channel on their spring and autumn migrations; often in great numbers. I've seen them 'drop in' on Steep Holm to feed for half an hour or so and then vanish, only to be followed a short while later by another itinerant crowd passing through, and then another. . . Another possibility is that it derives from 'swall' meaning "an agitated mass of water" (OED).*

[30] *Tony Thomas told Chris Richards of Weston Museum that his grandfather built the shrimp house and that it was in use up until the 1950s. In the late 1800s a man could earn up to £3 a week fishing shrimps; more than three times a labouring wage.*

Walking eastwards, the land rises to the south in narrow, stepped terraces; as though the grass had been grooved.[31] Cattle are often grazed here, browsing along the ridge, staring abstractedly out to sea. Below us, because it's low tide, Rosie and I can make out the remains of the stakes which once supported the shrimp and stall nets; they're still lined up in the mud, patiently on parade, despite long abandonment.[32]

Back at the National Trust car-park there is a third way up to Middle Hope. The track behind the perimeter trees is a private road leading to Woodspring House which stands, beneath a splendid Monterey cypress, on the southern slopes of Middle Hope - I remember the house once serving morning coffee and afternoon tea in its 'Refreshment Rooms'. Footpath access along this road arrives at steps which carry you up to a stile and onto the Middle Hope plateau, where an insistent view awaits. From the hilltop stile, the pathway follows a diagonal course east, across fields and broken walls, to the largest of the Middle Hope bays - also perfectly accessible along the cliff top from the shrimp-house, but it's so good to have a choice!

[31]According to Chris Richards of North Somerset Museum, these are sometimes called 'terracettes', brought about by landslip on a hillside. It's a natural process.

[32]It's curious how durable these sticks stuck in Severn mud are. I've seen insubstantial tree branches, stabbed into the River Brue estuary to mark the navigable channel, survive for years - despite ferocious currents.

The bay is a substantial 250 metre scoop out of the hillside, its two sister coves lining up in etched, easterly succession beyond it. The soft, cropped grass seems moulded to the landscape and meets the light grey pebbles of the bays with dark curves of storm-stranded bladder-wrack. Warm and sheltered on a summer's day, I've been coming here for as long as I can remember[33] - just to wander along a beautiful, undulating coastline or maybe pick blackberries in the autumn. Even, perhaps, an illicit summer night party, with a bonfire of driftwood on the beach below the Swallow Cliffs. I've always felt each of the four coves deserved its own name but, other than 'Swallow Cliff Bay' for the most westerly, they remain chastely untitled. The larger, middle bay describes an almost perfect semicircle, with quite a steep incline and narrow terraces of slipped land forming a natural amphitheatre - with the Severn Sea and the Welsh coast as backdrop. There are no defunct volcanoes here.

[33]*At the age of 15, working for 'H.Walsh, Commercial Photographer'*
during the summer holidays, I entered an 'enlarged photograph'
of Middle Hope in an Eagle comic competition. It didn't get anywhere.

Above the bay, the track leads to a stone-walled cattle enclosure and, although the gates are often unlocked, the footpath actually proceeds over a nearby wall by means of an 'A' framed wooden ladder. From here, the Middle Hope ridge rises above thickets of briar, hawthorn and gorse which crowd these north facing slopes, with the farm-track continuing eastwards beside a long stone wall. Rosie and I catch the tower of Woodspring Priory, some half a mile away, peeking over the capping stones. A short distance along the ridge we break downhill to a grassy basin that leads to the remaining two, west-facing coves. Both of these look very much like the bay at Swallow Cliff - not surprising since they share a similar geology. For here, the volcanoes return with great, lumpen outcrops of khaki coloured rock; the 'tuff' formed from settling volcanic ash. However, unlike Swallow Cliff, there is no lava formation - just the debris of those preadamic explosions.[34]

From the Middle Hope ridge,
looking to Woodspring Priory

[34]*During the Carboniferous period (360-295 million years ago) bursts of volcanic activity went on for some time, each followed by periods of calm. This allowed strata of limestone and sandstone to form, with the bands of volcanic ash (tuff) in between - this is especially evident at Swallow Cliff. A rather 'younger' Carboniferous volcanic zone is found at Spring Cove, near Birnbeck on Worlebury Hill, where lava is far more in evidence. Here, the molten rock, extruded from volcanic vents, solidified as black basalt together with pillow lavas that cooled under water. It appears to have been more violent too - in the Worlebury cliffs there are zones of crushed rocks and smashed limestones ('breccia') which are mixed with the pillow basalts.*

To the east, the Middle Hope ridge ends at St. Thomas's Head; somewhere that's always been rather mysterious to me - in an Enid Blyton sort of way. The Ministry of Defence secures this foreland behind high fences - inaccessible but very tidy, with manicured lawns and serviced by the surprise of a private, tarmacadam road from Woodspring Priory. Viewed from the sea, there are a couple of neat Nissen huts accompanied by a collection of their modern Portakabin equivalents - all perched on the bluff overlooking a north jetty and a west pier, with various gantries offshore.[35] From the middle bay to St. Thomas's Head there are low steep cliffs which, with dense bordering scrub, makes access to the shoreline difficult . This part of Middle Hope is reckoned to have "evidence of ancient field systems", although all Rosie and I can see are some broken walls set into sloping pasture.[36] The land then falls sharply away into Woodspring Bay and the levels of Wick St. Lawrence and Kingston Seymour.

Out in the Channel, the low tide has revealed the Langford Grounds, a golden sand-bank patterning, arcing beyond Woodspring Bay and reaching out, some 3 km, to the stumpy promontory of Clevedon's Wain's Hill. The Bristol Channel was defying its reputation as 'a brown stream', reflecting back the quiet blue of a summer sky.

[35] *This place was used for weapons' testing during the Second World War,*
and Woodspring Bay since the mid-1800s - it's always been 'off-limits'.
I used to watch various inscrutable goings-on through my telescopic gunsight up on Worlebury Hill.
The unexploded shells, depth charges and mines that were forever turning up in Sand
and Woodspring Bays just confirmed my imaginings.

[36] *Although now largely discounted, E.G.F. Routledge speculated that*
a defensive encampment existed at Middle Hope,
with a complex of earthworks, ditches, ramparts and cultivated strips.

Chapter Four

WOODSPRING

River Banwell estuary, low tide

Not so many years ago, the coastal stroll over Middle Hope came to a halt on the grassland above St. Thomas's Head. Stern 'no trespassing' notices[37] forbade progress to the shore and, with similar restrictions to the fields surrounding Woodspring Priory, the monastery buildings were always, tantalisingly, just out of reach as well. But now (since 1993), there is a footpath leading, through a narrow stretch of coastal woodland, down to the beach behind the headland. This area, where the diminutive River Banwell has its muddy estuary, is more saltmarsh than beach. Arriving here on a hot midday in June, it has taken on a soft blue haze. The Sea lavender is in full flower, taking up every available space along the shoreline and yielding a pervasive, honeyed scent.[38] The river channel visible from the shoreline is actually a creek whose origins arise in the Sand and Kewstoke Rhynes which drain the levels below

Middle Hope and join the River Banwell at its estuary. The 'real' River Banwell lies hidden behind a defensive embankment which protects the low-lying land for half a kilometre inland. The creek is home to a few dinghys and small motor boats, a rickety wooden jetty negotiating (at low tide) an uncertain way over the wide, muddy, western bank. But this can never be an easy place to set sail from; something to which a scatter of decaying craft (one had an estate agent's 'For Sale' notice) above the high-water line gave testimony.

Sea lavender

[37]*In extreme youth, I was convinced 'Trespassers will be Prosecuted' meant summary execution.*

[38]*Sea lavender, (Limonium vulgare), normally reckoned to be odourless but positively fragrant on this June morning. The small lilac-blue flowers, arranged in 2 rows along short stems above a clump of grey-green leaves, are 'everlasting' when dried. Its ground-up root was used as an astringent. Its rarer cousin Rock sea lavender (L. binervosum), paler flowers on longer stems, thrives on the Middle Hope cliffs but grows especially freely on Steep Holm. Both are closely related to the beautiful pink flowered Thrift.*

The footpath travels the drier zone below the trees, following the direction of the creek beside the fissured, marshy ground. It encircles a large saltwater pond[39] - full of fish trapped, we suppose, by the retreat of the last spring tides. They scurry close to the surface, in dark, wheeling turns, searching for an escape to the sea - a long way off at this low tide. Across the pond, we can make out the tower of the priory through the trees and it's here an embankment meets the headland, securing the Woodspring land from the sea. About here too, the path divides, with the choice of a short detour through the fields or continuing alongside the inlet to where the creek ends at a clyce bridge called Hucker's Bow,[40] controlling the flow of water from the rhynes.

The path surmounts the dyke and arrives at a small National Trust carpark - along with a whiff of the piggery close by. The gravel track then accompanies the Sand Rhyne on a short journey to Collum Lane and Woodspring Priory, where a small terrace of 19th century cottages fronts the road. Between them and the priory's boundary wall, a small iron kissing-gate leads into the priory grounds. Throughout its ecclesiastical existence the priory was known as 'Worspring' but, and for no very obvious reason, sometime in the early 17th century the name 'Woodspring' emerged.

Woodspring Priory and the infirmary, early summer

[39] *The pond is man-made, excavated by Avon Wildlife. When I revisited the pond in winter there was no sign of the fish. Perhaps they'd been nobbled by herons.*

[40] *A 'bow' is a small, arched bridge and 'clyce' is Somerset for a tidal sluice. The clyce's construction is often an opportunity for a bridge over the waterway.*

Worspring Priory, despite a press of modern farm buildings, holds on to an atmosphere of monastic quietude. The high Perpendicular tower imposes an inescapable solemnity and looks out over the wide expanse of the Kewstoke levels to Worlebury Hill. Even now, the place feels remote and withdrawn. As Rosie and I cross the southern grounds, the buildings are illuminated by early afternoon sunshine, Dundry stone shining back yellow amber. The first building we arrive at from this approach is the Infirmary with the remains of a spiral staircase, like a gigantic fossil, in its south wall. A further kissing-gate, next to the infirmary's east wall, leads us into the east orchard, the priory tower rising over 60 ft above us. Much of this area once housed a whole range of monastery buildings including the chancel (all razed following the Dissolution of the Monasteries in 1536) whose outline we can still make out on the tower's east wall. We enter the base of the tower into the church's crossing, through a small door from where the chancel once stood and where its eastern archway is now filled with buff, ashlar stone. Sunlight enters through a high south window whose tracery shadow follows the hour over the crossing floor. This sunlight seems to emphasise the gloom of the north aisle which, along with its high windows, has lost its fan-vaulted ceiling (the vaulting in the crossing was restored in the 19th century). This area now contains an exhibition of Worspring discoveries and restoration work. If you're alone, watch out for the light that comes on suddenly and makes you jump - it's as though someone's entered, silently, from somewhere else. It is thought the north aisle was, possibly, the home of the 'Becket Reliquary' which found its way into the north wall of St. Paul's Church in Kewstoke after the Dissolution (see Special Page).[41]

[41]Sometime after the Dissolution in 1536, five of the priory's choir stalls were taken to St. Martin's Church in Worle, while the beautiful carved stone pulpit at Wick St. Lawrence Church may also have come from Woodspring. According to antiquarian Phil Quinn, a local legend holds that blackbirds around Woodspring sing differently, retaining in their song the holy music once heard at the priory. Up until the mid-1970s, the priory was surrounded by pollarded elms - they were all lost to Dutch elm disease.

The Crossing, Woodspring Priory, morning sunlight

Back in the crossing, what was the west arch leading to the church's nave, is now a wall harbouring a sturdy Victorian door. Passing through, like Alice, we are suddenly in another place. This is the comfortable smoking-room of a gentleman's club![42] Light fills the room from a great, mullioned window, illuminating a wide fireplace, a capacious table set with books, 'deep rose' walls - something of the romance of Woodspring seems to be here. So, I'm not surprised to discover that William Lisle Bowles,[43] Samuel Taylor Coleridge's early poetic mentor, had been affected by the priory's atmosphere:

> But mark that hill
> Where Kewstoke seems to creep into the sea
> Thy abbey, Woodspring, rose. Wild is the spot;
> And there three mailed murderers retired,
> To the last point of land. There they retired,
> And there they knelt upon the ground, and cried,
> Bury us 'mid the waves, where none may know
> The whispered secret of a deed of blood!

[42]In 1895, a Bristol surgeon, James Greig Smith discovered Woodspring
("It needs a poet to understand the charm of the place.") and, with seven friends
(they called themselves 'The Octave of golfing canons'), founded a golf club in the priory
with its 'links' up on Middle Hope. The clubroom was decorated in a High Gothic Victorian
style and they seem to have been a jocular bunch. In a collection of his essays,
Smith describes a moment in a golf match when eating shrimps took precedence -
"Later on the two interrupted their match at the shrimper's hut,
and were found eating shrimps as fast as the shrimp-boiler could unshell them.
They cheerfully let two couples pass them. This, they were told, put them out
of the competition for the handicap sweep. After examining their cards they said they submitted,
but they thought it a harsh rule"! The club did not long survive Greig Smith's early death in 1898.
Chris Crook, Curator of Woodspring, told me there have been times when he has caught the
scent of cigars in the old clubroom. ('Woodspring' by James Greig Smith)

[43]I mention Bowles in our Weston-super-Mare book - his father was pastor of Uphill church from 1769-86.
His 'plain and simple' poetic style greatly influenced both Coleridge and William Wordsworth.

In fact, the nave was divided and used as a family residence almost as soon as the priory was given up by the canons, and a similar fate overtook the north aisle whose fan-vault ceiling was "quarried out" (as Curator, Chris Crook, puts it). In the late 17th century, Woodspring was aquired by the Smyth Pigott family and it's around this time the farmhouse was built. They were also responsible for repairs to the tower and the fan-vault ceiling of the crossing. The wonderful Monastic Barn[44] and the infirmary have survived, almost intact from the 15th century, simply because they continued to have an agricultural purpose. Against the barn's eastern wall is the spring which may have contributed to the priory's name. Fifteen stone steps spiral down through the Lias limestone - built to reach the variable levels of the spring water.[45]

[44]Woodspring Priory also owned a tithe-barn in Worle - next to St. Martin's Church.
By the early 1800s it was a ruin, but in 1866 it was rebuilt as a school which survives to this day.
The buttresses of the old barn still support the building along Church Road.

[45]The well is vulnerable to drought. Even in ordinary conditions, if pumped dry, it will take 3 days to refill. Later wells (to the north and west of the buildings) served the farmhouse kitchen, the cider cellar and the laundry.

A map in the 'clubhouse' room shows, when it came on the market in 1928, the Woodspring Priory Estate consisted of: Middle Hope, St. Thomas's Head, Sand Point and a considerable chunk of Sand Bay - including Sandpoint and Sandbay farms and pockets of land all over the place. After the sale (which saved it from becoming a holiday village) Woodspring Priory served as a farm once again until 1968, when it and its precious adjoining coastline were secured by The National Trust. The Landmark Trust aquired the main priory buildings in 1969, with some land round about - it's a hugely popular place to stay. The monastic barn and the coast remain in the care of The National Trust.

The Monastic Barn, Woodspring Priory

The Becket Reliquary

The Becket Seal

Three West country noblemen were involved in splattering the brains of Thomas a Becket
about the altar of Canterbury Cathedral in 1170. Almost immediately,
a cult of 'Becket's Blood' arose, with wooden cups of the vital fluid strung up around the
Cathedral altar. Later, rather more durable vessels of earthenware and lead were used.
Inevitably, the blood became endowed with magical healing properties and vials containing
much diluted saintly gore - 'Canterbury Water' - were sold to the faithful who visited the
Cathedral shrine. Such was its power that any amount of disease and mortifications could be
cured. It must have become an important source of revenue and,
in order to keep the money rolling in, it was watered down to homeopathic dilutions.
Francis Knight tells the extraordinary story of a Canterbury pilgrim returning home through
Rochester and unable to find a bed for the night. Eventually, one hostelry took him in,
whereupon, the town caught fire. By holding up his sample of Canterbury Water
on a hayfork towards the fire, the pilgrim's guest-house was saved.
"The fire, as if fearing a contrary element, turned aside."!! Meanwhile,
the rest of Rochester burned to the ground.

Continued

The original Worspring chapel, built in the early 13th century, was dedicated to the 'The Blessed Martyr, Thomas' by William de Courtenay, who had gained title to the land by marriage to a descendant of Reginald Fitz Urse; one of the knights who killed Becket. A group of St Augustinian canons and their prior took up occupation "to pray for the salvation" of William and his family.

Early on, the priory was fairly impoverished, but by the 15th century it embarked on the construction of a new church (complete with a tower in the Somerset Perpendicular style), and other works including a tithe-barn and an infirmary. The north aisle was added in the early 16th century. All this came to abrupt halt with the Dissolution of the Monasteries in 1536. However; it was not unexpected and the prior, with his canons, had time to prepare - they sold land and farms before the final break with Rome.

In 1849, during repairs to St. Paul's Church in Kewstoke, masons discovered a hollowed-out piece of sculpted stone containing a wooden vessel stained with blood. It's very likely this was a 'Becket Reliquary', taken from its home in the new north aisle at Worspring to be hidden during the days before the final orders for suppression came through. (Support for it being a 'true relic' comes from the priory's 13th century seal; it shows an assassin's sword and St. Thomas's head accompanied by a small cup). The monks must have hidden it hoping, one day, they would be able to return. They never did. But in 1970, on December 29th, 900 years after Thomas a Becket's murder, the Bishop of Bath and Wells held a re-hallowing service at the priory. The St. Paul's Church reliquary was brought from the Somerset Museum in Taunton for the special day - returning home, after over 400 years, in a way the canons never could.

Chapter Five

WICK ST. LAWRENCE AND PUXTON

The Ebdon Bow

In the 1950s, Wick St. Lawrence was a comfortable bike ride from my home
on the top of Worlebury Hill. I could scoot down, and up, Spring Hill in Worle,
past St. Martin's Church, on through the old hillside village to Gunning's Stores at the
top of The Scaurs. Then, it was left, down past the old forge to the Ebdon Road, up the
slight rise near Castle Batch, and along the flat, narrow-laned, rhyne-land to Wick.[46]
Going that way today, Wick St. Lawrence totters on the brink of suburbia; North Worle
breathing down its neck, held back by the slow flow of the humble Banwell River.
The road still arrives at the hamlet of Ebdon to congratulate the diminutive river with a
handsome stone bridge (the Ebdon Bow), before twisting the final few yards to Wick.

[46]*The name 'Wick' crops up frequently in Somerset - there's even one down the road: West Wick, near Worle. According to
Knight, all the Wicks are on low ground and the name may derive from the Saxon 'Wic' - a dwelling, or when close to
a navigable river, from the Norse 'Wik' - a creek. The Banwell River was once called the Wick or the Old Yeo.*

Paul's canoe at New Bow Sluice

The Banwell River begins life as a collection of springs at the centre of its namesake village and where they once filled a large pool below the Church.[47] The course of the Banwell has been pushed about over the centuries and now runs in a series of straight 'cuts' through the levels, receiving, as it goes, ditch and rhyne water. From the Ebdon Bow,[48] it's possible to take a canoe towards the sea and, on one occasion I and my good friend Paul Cossham did just that. Pushing out from beneath a crowd of sprawling willows, we sidled below the bridge, passing between Banfield and Ebdon farms where the stream barely moved and the water's surface was thick with duckweed.[49] It was hard work paddling through this vegetable broth and curious to be below the sea-level pastures. Reeds grew high on either side, with bright white umbels of angelica and hemlock, and brilliant splashes of yellow flag irises. Once in a while, a duck broke cover, possibly protecting its young, but appearing trapped by a failure of imagination. Half-flying 10 yards ahead of us, flapping and flailing, trailing through the duckweed for ages, until it eventually dived back amongst the reeds. Cows assumed complete disinterest, scarcely raising their heads, as we paddled sedately by.

[47] *Through an Act of Parliament, and despite local protests, the Banwell springs were capped in 1915 and the pool slowly dried up. The water became part of the Weston Water Company's supply. The old pool was filled in and became the village bowling green where, I understand, it is still possible to hear the flow of spring water. It was said the Banwell church bells sounded sweetest when heard across the waters of the pond. (Local historians: Joan and Stan Rendell)*

[48] *Paul and Hilary Cossham's 'Discovery' canoe is of Native Canadian design, though made in the USA.*

[49] *19th century Weslyan Methodist fervour really took hold in Wick. The villagers built their own chapel and were congratulated on the absence of beer-houses. Farmer Gould of Banfield Farm was especially taken up with religious enthusiasm and poured his excellent cider into the Banwell River and severely inebriating the ducks. (John Bailey)*

Flag iris, River Banwell

Gradually the river opened out, with clear runs of weed-free water. Middle Hope appeared, the Woodspring Priory tower just visible through breaks in the reeds. After a mile or so of waterway, the journey ended at a large clyce gate (the New Bow Sluice), but before that the Banwell had a surprise in store, for it widens into a broad lagoon complete with a small island. Arriving, we disturbed a family of swans who made a dignified escape down a small backwater close to the dam. On landing the canoe amongst the reeds close to the clyce, it was easy to clamber onto the raised bankside. From the bow, the almost empty (it was low tide), muddy channel of the Banwell curved away to St. Thomas's Head and the sea. To the north-west lay the protective embankments known as the Wick Warths[50] with Clevedon just nodding over the horizon.

[50] *Warths (Old English) - seaboard land reclaimed by the construction of an outer sea-wall, leaving the original sea-defence some distance inland. The warths lie wide and open between the two sea-walls, rather different to the older and smaller, hedged fields inland. (Keith Gardner). Fuller account in Chapter 6.*

Despite the obtrusion of Weston-cum-Worle and despite never having had a post
office, a pub or a village shop, Wick St. Lawrence maintains a strong identity. Rosie and
I arrive, with a final turn in the road, outside St. Lawrence's Church. The church stands
proud on what seems to be, an isolated hillock, bounded by a high, ivy-capped, stone
wall and fine iron gates. After the constriction of the country lanes, this area before
the church feels open and yet sheltered, with a magisterial yew tree (reckoned
as being at least as old as the 15th century church) filling the western part of the
churchyard. To the north, the churchyard looks out over orchards and open fields
towards Woodspring Bay. A fine, though disfigured, village cross stands on a small green

opposite the church; the shaft raised up on
five ascending octagonal stone platforms -
all it lacks is its crosshead; lopped off in
Cromwell's time. The cross stands at the
entrance to School Lane,[51] where also
stands the medieval Church House,
once the centre of brewing and
revelry! Unsportingly, it was
converted to the village poorhouse,
then fell into general ruination,
to be rescued as a private house in
recent times.

St. Lawrence's Church, in its
present guise, is mainly 15th century,
but Christianity had been served by
older, smaller buildings long before
that - remnants of which crop up in
various walls around the village. It is built mainly
of pink/grey Lias limestone combined with other limestones
and sandstones from the locality; these were used during a major 19th
century restoration made necessary after the church was struck by lightning in 1791.[52]

[51]According to Linda Jenkins of The Old Schoolhouse, School Lane was very much the heart of the village. But, over the
years, several houses became dilapidated and were pulled down and another was destroyed by fire - although it was
rebuilt closer to the main road (Cedar Cottage). In the late 18th century, the Schoolhouse itself had replaced a
medieval curate's house and a building thought to be a monk's cell - both were damp and unhealthy; so their
Reverends, preferring the more commodious accommodation at Congresbury, journeyed to Wick by horse and carriage.

[52]This was a catastrophic event which even hit the pages of the London Chronicle on January 14th 1791; "The Thunderbolt
struck the Weather Cock of the Tower, and very much damaged the Pinnacle, entered the West Window, and took its course into
the body of the Church, scorched the Pulpit Cloth, and cracked the Pulpit which is built with Stone, and very much injured
the whole of the Fabric. The damage is estimated at three hundred pounds." Cracks appeared in the tower which was
reinforced with iron bands but, despite some repair work, over the next 60 years the church began to fall apart.

Unsurprisingly, since this is Somerset, the windows are in the Perpendicular style. The modest tower is surmounted by a magnificent weather cock with a great golden tail - which must surely have attracted that lightning strike; it's amazing it has survived. Being within comfortable range, the plume is wonderfully puckered by the arrows of small boys and other dead-shots who have found its splendour, and the temptation to set it spinning, irresistible. The tower has a peal of six bells; the three oldest were cast in 1655, the newest (the treble) in 1921 originally for a church in Liverpool, now demolished. It was hung and dedicated at St. Lawrence's in 1994, after villagers had raised the money to buy it.

The pulpit, St. Lawrence's Church

Inside the church, coming upon the beautiful stone pulpit is something unexpected.[53] Picked out by the light from the south facing windows, poised upon the finest of carved pillars, its delicate, Gothic detailing somehow allows it to defy gravity. One of the memorial tablets in the church (now resting in the church porch) underscores our closeness to the the sea and its dangers. Rather battered, with a singular use of capitals and running out of space towards the end, it reads:-

> "To the Memory of James Morss, of this parish, Yeoman, who dy'd
> November ye 25th, 1730, aged 38 years.
>
> Save me O God, the Mighty Waters role
> With near Approaches, even to my Soul:
> Far from Dry Ground, mistaken in my Course,
> I stick in Mire, brought hither by my Horse.
> Thus vain I cry'd to God, Who only Saves:
> In Death's Cold Pit I lay ore whelmed w'th waves."

Even today, people misjudge the speed of the incoming tide over the mud flats, and lives are still lost.

The road from Wick curves past the orchards of Icelton and the high Black poplars (rattling their leaves) to Bourton. Nearby, the Weston, Clevedon & Portishead Light Railway (WCPLR) once rattled as well; north-eastwards over the fields, to bridge the River Yeo at what's called 'Tutshill Ear'.[54] There was also an important jetty here (you can still see the sad remains), where coal from South Wales was unloaded, to be taken to the 'coaling-point' at Clevedon station or the town's gas works. Wick St. Lawrence even managed its own station building. It came complete with a waiting room and a booking hall - all packed into something not much bigger than a garden shed!

[53]Following the Dissolution of the Monasteries in 1536, Woodspring Priory was bought by a Bristol merchant, William Carr. He died soon after and it seems likely his son and heir, John Carr, (who became Lord to the Manors of both Congresbury and Wick St. Lawrence), arranged the pulpit's relocation from Woodspring to Wick. (Linda Jenkins)

[54]More correctly 'yere' - yet another name for a sluice allowing water to flow out and not in; same linguistic root as 'weir'. See also Hook's Ear. (Keith Gardner)
The present sluice is of recent construction and beyond this point the River Yeo ceases to be tidal.

Wick St. Lawrence is isolated from its sister village of Puxton by a conspiracy of motorway, railway and road. The Bourton lane threads its way across the first two, so as to arrive at the former Palmer's Elm pub[55] (now, confusingly, a Chinese restaurant) on the A370. Then it's left, first right between the willows, and over the 'weak' bridge that crosses the Oldbridge River. Puxton remains a fairly compact village, although it has given up its remote, Northmarsh character through post-war house building. Puxton Lane loops south of the village and it is from here that you can get the best view of its extraordinary little church.[56] Here is the leaning tower of Puxton - the top tilts a good metre (about 10 degrees) from the vertical - emphasised, from where we are standing, by the very flatness of the field before it. The cause is self-evident; this is boggy, peaty ground and many churches on the Somerset Levels show the same inclination. Indeed, in 1866 a church tower at Hewish (less than a mile away) only got half way up before it fell down! They didn't try again.

<hr />

[55] *The former pub-sign showed a man hanged from a high elm.*

[56] *There are records of a church at Puxton since 947 AD, although the present St. Saviour's is early 14th century. Despite some 16th and 19th century work, it holds on to its primitive character - the Victorian slates cover roof timbers made up from "bare tree trunks". The pyramid lead roof of the tower sports a remarkable collection of 'footprints' carved into the soft metal, with initials and dates of the benign perpetrators within their shoe's outlines (eg. MM 1809) - sort of early graffiti (Joan Rendell).*

The Legend of John Crock

(from a talk given by C.W.Dymond in 1905)

The Northmarsh can be a strange, misty place; a shadowland where folk become confused and fearfully lost. Sea-fog hangs low over the wet land and will-o'-the-wisp ignitions add to the domain of awful mystery...

John Crock was a ploughman working for a farmer in Wick St. Lawrence. While crossing a stream one evening, on his way home, marsh-gas from the saltings took the form of a black dog. The animal spoke and told the petrified John Crock that the dog's master was The Devil and, to appease him, John Crock must steal grain from his farmer's barn. John did as he was bid, but the next night the gas took on the form of a black horse with a single eye in the centre of its forehead. It too claimed to be the Devil's agent, but this time it required John to concoct evidence against the wife of a local parish priest. She was taken as a witch and burned at the stake.

Over the months, the vapours took on increasingly sinister forms, driving poor John Crock to further violent deeds: setting a farm on fire, killing cattle and finally, in an act of desperate insanity, murdering his beloved wife and only son. Grief-stricken and overcome with remorse, he threw himself from the Swallow Cliffs at Middle Hope.

Many years later, a stonemason from Weston-super-Mare was so affected by this sad and dreadful story that he carved out a tablet of stone with a verse telling the tale. He placed it above the cliff at Middle Hope from where John Crock had leapt into oblivion. In 1818, William Lisle Bowles (whom I mention in the Woodspring chapter) was walking the headlands in very wet and stormy weather (he complained of his breeches being soaked through), when, with some amazement, he came across the inscribed stone. Being a poet and having a pen and paper handy, he made a note of what was written:-

Continued

Neath Swallowcliffe

Where cold seas role

John Crock met death

Pray for his soul

Devil, black dog and one-eyed stallion

Trouble him no more - his body's carrion.

If Bowles hadn't passed by, that part of the story would have been lost, for three years later two local men, suffering a surfeit of cider, threw the tablet from the cliff top, where it smashed to pieces on the rocks below.

Chapter Six

THE WARTHS OF WICK AND KINGSTON SEYMOUR

The mouth of the Yeo, high tide

Much of the coast between Wick St. Lawrence and Clevedon is difficult to get at, for much of it is in private ownership - right up to the outer sea-walls. Also, the River Yeo effectively divides these lowlands in two, with the first effective bridge lying some way inland, at Congresbury. All this means the only public footpath access to the shoreline is from Clevedon Pill or the footpaths off the Lower Strode Road. There are other ways, but you have to ask. Hopefully, efforts to create a coastal path will succeed and improve access all round.

At Wick St. Lawrence, a track called Muddy Lane takes you to the fields behind the sea-walls, close to the mouth of the River Yeo. Here, the course of the Yeo, or its streamlet tributaries, has changed, for there are deep, grassed-over gulleys crossing the fields - the ghosts of redundant watercourses. Standing high above the river mouth, we could see the embankment separated into two enclosing arms - one is the front-line sea-wall faced with stone and bitumen, the other, running parallel to it about 150m inland, is a high grass bank probably demarcating the position of ancient sea-defences.[57] The area between the walls constitutes the Wick Warth; a substantial acreage of reclaimed pastureland running westwards some 1.5 km to the mouth of the River Banwell, below St. Thomas's Head. In effect, it forms a long, shallow valley and, when we were there in midwinter, sheep were grazing in sheltered comfort; despite the blast of the cold, north wind we were feeling at our backs, up on the high sea-wall.

On the northerly side of the Yeo's mouth, the Kingston Seymour Warth is made up in the same way; the two walls running parallel north-east for 2 km or so, as far as a small muddy creek called Kingston Pill or Hook's Ear. From thereon, the walls come together to form a single wide embankment that runs up to Clevedon.

[57]*Silt and the Severn Estuary go hand in hand. Not long after the original sea-defences were constructed (possibly by the Romans) silt (mud) would have begun to accumulate on the wall's seaward side. Indeed, the same thing is happening now - assisted by spartina grass (see chapter two)! Fences and stakes set into the mud would have accelerated the process and, although initially subject to recurring flood, the saltings would have eventually become useful summer pasture and worthy of an additional, outer sea-wall. This land, moderately higher than the original meadows, is called a 'warth'. Much of this reclamation took place during the 17th century when there was pressure on pastureland - cattle were being brought to the district from as far away as Wales for fattening prior to market.*

You can get to the Kingston Warth down a wide track at the end of the village's Middle Lane. It brings you onto the sea-wall just south of Hook's Ear where the wall is quite a substantial structure, a double rise of bitumen coated stone interrupted by a wide, concrete terrace. When Rosie and I were there, it was a cold February morning with the promise of snow from the east. An extreme, low tide had exposed extensive sand-banks on the Langford Grounds offshore. In the middle distance, picked out in yellow winter sunlight, were the exploded hulks of two ships, beaten to bits by the weapons testing of the Ministry of Defence. These sad 'target vessels' were the undignified remains of the Steam Ships Fernwood and Staghound. Still recognisably boatlike, they were splayed out on Severn Estuary mud, disembowelled, their boiler entrails for all to see.

The target ships, Woodspring Bay

The importance of the sea-wall's integrity cannot be overemphasised - without it, much of the seaward land would revert to saltmarsh. According to Ken Stuckey, maintenance of the old walls had, for centuries, been the responsibility of local farmers and landowners. Each individual took care of a proportionate section of the wall, designated by a marker called a 'dolestone' on which were carved a number and the farmer's initials. The sections were measured out in 'lugs' (about 5m),[58] 'spades' and 'lengths'. Once a year, the walls were inspected by a body of 12 men (His Majesties' Commissioners of Sewers and Dykes Reeves) who rode on horseback from the New Bow Cut at Wick St. Lawrence, along the sea-wall to the embankments of the River Yeo and from there to Yatton church ending up, inevitably, in the Prince of Orange pub. Local sea-wall responsibility continued up until 1938, when it was taken over by the Somerset Rivers Board.

Kingston Wharth (with cow)

[58]*The December 1981 Banwell Society of Archaeology Newsletter describes a*
field trip with Kingston Seymour, farmer-historian Ken Stuckey.
At that time Ken kept the family dolestone in the boot of his car.
The term 'lug' may have derived from 'apple-lugs' - long poles used to knock apples
from trees (Phyllis Cram & Joan Rendell).
In Yatton, dolestones are known as 'meer' stones.

Beside the Kingston Warth, at the Yeo's mouth, are excavated ponds created during the consolidation of the sea defences in 1987. Known as Blake's Pools, the largest, which is contiguous with the river embankment, connects directly with the Yeo through a breach in the wall and empties completely at low tide. A bird-hide has been constructed at the seaward end and looks down the length of the pond. Smaller pools, a little further inland, support a bountiful harvest of Common reeds, so clearly contain fresh water. While we were there, heifers grazed happily on the outer warth walls. Apparently, cattle and sheep can eat salt-sprayed grass without harm,[59] but (like us) drinking salt-water does them no good at all.

Trespassers with guns... will be shot?

The drainage ditches and rhynes of the north levels continue to be kept clear by the farmers - called 'keeching the rhynes' in the local parlance. Rhynes are keeched twice a year - first one side and then the other. The fields themselves are sectioned into extended humps, like corrugations, forming drainage grooves (known as 'grypes') from which the water runs off into the rhynes.[60] The rhynes gradually widen, eventually forming main watercourses called 'yeos' (although the term 'yeo' has now been confusingly appropriated by the River Yeo - formerly known as the Congresbury Yeo).

Throughout the Somerset Levels, the smaller rivers and water outflows are controlled by tidal sluices (often called clyces or yeres!) which close down as the tide rises preventing the influx of seawater. At low tide the sluice gates open and water flows out - a simple and very effective drainage system. In times of drought the sluice can be closed completely retaining water in the rhynes. Inland, flooding is also controlled by additional wall embankments forming barriers between adjacent marshy land. Some of these banks have extraordinary names like 'Gang Wall' and 'Wow Wall'; they also provide dry paths across flooded land.

[59]*John Rutter, 1829, was not too sure about this -*
"The occasional inundations to which these lands are subject,
render the herbage unpalatable to cattle, for a year or two afterwards,
and they produce offensive exhalations..."

[60]*Roland & Franky Griffin of Kingston Seymour told us the 'grype' was an ancient system*
of drainage but extremely effective; there are no pipes involved.
oland recalled a farmer who ploughed up the grypes in one field
which then became waterlogged and useless.
Keith Gardner considers the grypes (or gripes!) to be Romano-British in origin.

Defending the Sea-walls

Ensuring the sea-walls at Woodspring Bay are sound remains a never-ending task. Keeping the sea out of the coastal plains makes the creation of productive pasture possible and the development of the warths, a double barrier to a storm tide, has brought the bonus of extra acres of grazing land. But the tide isn't the sea-wall's only enemy; badger sets and mole tunnels, on the landward side, can weaken the structure enough for serious breaches to occur.

Up until the Second World War, whenever storms were anticipated, men known as 'watchers' were stationed at the walls. Stone, sandbags and tools were kept ready in huts close by, with the watchers on regular night patrols at times of high danger. A siren would be sounded should ever a breach occur.

Around the early 1900s, the Wick landowners employed Edward Thomas, a deaf-mute, to guard the Wick Warth walls. He spent much of his time in a small hut behind the sea-wall and was able to take immediate action whenever damage occurred. To build 30 yards of wall took 170 tons of stone and this was often brought by sea from Wain's Hill Quarry in Clevedon, or Uphill Quarry, south of Weston-super-Mare. Mariner Edmund Eglinton (see Kingston Seymour chapter) describes a Captain Leonard Smart (who came complete with peaked cap, gold earrings and white moustache) bringing stone from Uphill to the Kingston Seymour walls in his small trow *Jane,* which he kept berthed in the River Axe at Uphill. As Skipper Smart put it, the trow was sailed into position and then "dumpted" in the mud off Woodspring Bay and the stone unloaded over the side. Edward Thomas, in his time, would have helped to bring the stone ashore. He would also deal with dead animals washed up along the coast and it was his responsibility to bury them in the mud. During the First World War the corpse of a camel 'hove to' on the shore and Edward Thomas buried it. Half of Kingston and Wick came to watch.

In 1937 the Somerset Rivers Board took on the responsibility for the walls' upkeep and, more recently, the task has been assumed by the Environment Agency.

(I'm grateful to Linda Jenkins for much of the information in this section.)

Chapter Seven

CONGRESBURY AND THE RIVER YEO

The village cross, Congresbury

The village of Congresbury[61] lies some 8 km from the north Somerset coast
whereas the River Yeo (which forms the village's natural western boundary), by virtue
of its meanderings, takes more than double the distance to reach the sea. As mentioned
in the previous chapter, Congresbury's bridge is the first road crossing of the Yeo
between Weston-super-Mare and Clevedon, making the coast of the northern levels
relatively inaccessible and remote - an effect compounded by the excluding sweep
of the M5 motorway.

[61] *Still pronounced "Coomsbry" by many a local; ignoring the legend the name derives from St. Congar who
made a name for himself healing the sick, planting walking sticks and getting yew trees,
reclaiming marshland and, possibly, even being Welsh - all around AD 530.*

Despite the difficulties of sailing the lower reaches of the wandering Yeo, the river was once tidal and fairly navigable up to Congresbury - to its weir on the south-east outskirts of the village. Indeed, it's probable barges were getting up to Congresbury during the mid-18th century supplying a mill which had been adapted to the manufacture of iron rods.[62] Water mills producing flour had inhabited sites close to this part of river for centuries, right up to the late 1920s. It remains an area of industrial activity.

The historic importance of the Yeo, as a navigable channel, was reinforced by the discovery, in 1884, of the site of a substantial Roman villa on the north bank of the river, south of Kingston Seymour, at Wemberham.[63] There were even indications the villa had its own dock or boathouse. And, of course, a mere 1,500 years or so later, the good, old Weston, Clevedon & Portishead Light Railway had a significant jetty down-river at Tutshill Ear (ie: yere), about 3 km from the river mouth. These days the sluice gates at Tutshill make it impossible for boats to get any further up river - as well as virtually eliminating any direct tidal effect upstream. Even so, the high riverside embankments remain in place right up to the Congresbury Weir - just in case the Severn Sea should decide to get serious.

In spite of the frenetic Weston/Bristol road skimming past its western border, Congresbury retains an attractive collection of houses, shops and pubs close to St. Andrew's Church. The tall 15th century village cross still stands guard opposite the 'Ship & Castle' pub[64] at the entrance to Broad Street. It once stood several feet higher - two steps of its octagonal base have disappeared beneath the road!

[62] A 'slitting mill ' turned iron bars or plates into rods, part of the process of manufacturing nails.
(See Gill Bedingfield's account in 'Congresbury as 'twas'.)
Alex Cran describes the transport of coal, timber, ochre and stone, in and out of Congresbury via the Yeo.

[63] Ken Stuckey knew one of the 'watchmen' employed to guard the villa's excavations. He told Ken the watchmen sold off pieces of the villa's tessellated pavement for half-a-crown (12p) in the 1880s.

[64] The Ship & Castle got its name from the arms of the City of Bristol. Both the inn and the village cross were owned by the Bristol Municipal Charities. The inn was sold in 1954 and the cross given to the village's parish council in the 1970s.

St. Andrew's rectory

Walking down Broad Street and turning right into Paul's Causeway leads up to the church and past another stone cross - this time without a column. Behind the trees, to the east of St. Andrew's, stands the vicarage, a Regency house which is an extension to a much older rectory. It was built in 1477, and has an imposing two storey stone 'porch' standing out powerfully from the Gothic-windowed, whitewashed house. In the churchyard is a three ton granite cross commemorating the bravery of farmer Charles Hardwick who, in 1830, battled with a highwayman and won.[65]

[65]*In late October 1830, Charles Hardwick, a Congresbury farmer, was returning from Bristol market with £500 in gold sovereigns stowed in his saddlebags. A distant relation, Richard Hewlett, overtook him on the road and joined him on the journey. Close to Hardwick's farm, Hewlett suddenly drew out a pistol and shot Hardwick. It was a poor shot; Charles was only wounded in the shoulder and Hewlett took off - his second pistol had failed to fire. After a chase on horseback, Hardwick caught up with Hewlett on Congresbury bridge. Hewlett struck out with a spring-loaded dagger stabbing Hardwick in the chest. Despite this, the chase continued until Hewlett's horse shied at an approaching cart and, throwing its rider, allowed Hardwick to continue the battle until others came to his aid. Gravely injured, Farmer Hardwick was carried to the Ship & Castle Inn at Congresbury where, swerving between life and death, he slowly recovered from his wounds. Richard Hewlett, a most unsatisfactory highwayman, was found guilty of attempted murder and highway robbery, and sentenced to death. He was hanged at the County Gaol, Ilchester, in April the following year.*

The River Yeo, looking to St. Andrew's Church

The River Yeo is found behind the Ship & Castle Inn, flowing parallel to the
High Street. Crossed by a steel footbridge, it's a short walk to the Congresbury Weir.
Tumbling water is always hypnotic and Rosie and I were suitably transfixed.
For a moment, the Yeo seemed positively animated! - cascading into a deep, still pool.
But that burst of activity clearly consumed all its strength; immediately the river
resumed its laggardly ways and its torpid journey to the sea. Upstream from the
weir, the river loses its high embankments and, overflowing its boundaries, forms
ponds and pools jealously guarded by the Yeo Valley Flyfishers, while the footpath
becomes the 'Two Rivers Way', a designated trail to Wrington, the Chew Valley lakes
and along the River Chew to Keynsham in east Somerset.

There was a time, travelling from Weston on the A370, your arrival at Congresbury was marked by a road bridge crossing the famous Cheddar Valley Railway (The Strawberry Line)[66] that traced its way from Yatton through Axbridge, Cheddar and Wells. Whenever I pulled up on my bike at the crest of the bridge or going by on the bus, I could peer over the parapet down onto Congresbury Station. From where I stood, it always appeared a picture-book railway scene with high-gabled station buildings and tall chimneys, signals and a wide platform on the up-line. And, if I was lucky, a train would come chuffing through - steam whooshing up on either side of the bridge.

[66]*The trains were packed with people and strawberries during the season. Much of the fruit was bound for Wimbledon. I once found myself chugging off to Wells by mistake, having got on the wrong train at Bristol. It was a very amiable diversion, but I had to get the bus back to Weston. The line closed in 1963 and the beautiful station was demolished in 1968 - from today's perspective, an inexplicable vandalism. The road bridge followed some years later.*

The Weston, Clevedon and Portishead Light Railway (deceased)

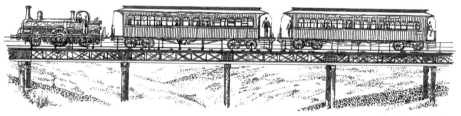

On the River Yeo bridge

Referred to, rather scabrously, as the 'WC & Pee', this small, independent, Somerset railway always maintained a special place in the affections of its travellers. However; it was never quite taken seriously and, despite the many years since its closure, it still raises a quiet smile. The line started life in 1885 when an Act of Parliament permitted the construction of a Tramway between Weston and Clevedon - by 1899 this had been upgraded to a Light Railway. From the start there were financial hiccups which slowed the initial work from Weston and it was 1907 before the line made it to Portishead. Two years later, it was in receivership and taken over by its main creditor, The Excess Insurance Company.

Continued

There were some 19 stations and halts along a line that made its way between Weston, Worle Town, Wick St. Lawrence (with its jetty and bridge over the River Yeo), Kingston Road, Clevedon, Walton-in-Gordano, Black Rock Quarry and Portishead. Many of the halts were milk collecting points with a raised platform for the churns and sentry-box cubicles for passengers. Whenever the trains didn't run or the service was especially infrequent, farmers used a hand propelled rail cart (like a scene from a silent movie) to get their milk to market.

The jetty at Wick St Lawrence was constructed in 1913 with high hopes of attracting seaborne trade. Sadly, the only regular business was coal from South Wales and that only came every month or so. The railway company had its own sailing barges for a time. One, the 'Lily', came to a sad end. Having set off from Newport in January 1929, with 30 tons of coal, she began taking water. Despite hours of desperate pumping (during which the captain collapsed from exhaustion) the 'Lily' turned over and sank, Captain Betteridge and crewman Jack Hunter diving for their lives at the last moment (Grahame Farr).

The railway company had hoped to extend the line right into Weston's main street, the Boulevard, and the rails were partly laid. But it wasn't to be and Westonians had to make do with a horse-drawn omnibus for the last bit of the journey. The Weston station was situated at the northern end of Ashcombe Road. The station building, with its curved, corrugated iron roof, was rather novel for its time and the style was repeated at Clevedon. The Clevedon station was the company headquarters; home to its offices, repair workshops, carriage and engine sheds and it was where the locomotives took on most of their coal and water. There was also a loop line to the Clevedon Gas Works and an important spur connection with the Great Western Railway - although GWR was always rather disapproving of its rural cousin.
Clearly, the old WC&P didn't quite come up to scratch!

Beyond Clevedon, the line made a steady climb through the beautiful Gordano valley, passing by the charming rustic shelter of Walton Park halt - the highest point on the line. Along this section there were several connecting spurs to quarries (Conygar and Black Stone) that used the railway to transport their stone.

Continued

After a journey of nearly 14 miles from Weston, the line terminated at the Portishead station - close to what is still called Station Road. The station building, sheltered by high elms, came complete with a ladies' room and maintained the Walton Park timbered rustication - although the rural calm was shattered somewhat by the presence of Mustad's nail factory (which had its own siding) on the opposite side of the track.

As well as its steam locomotives, the railway was rather innovative in having petrol engine railcars; these carried a lot of the regular passenger work and were cheap and easy to maintain. The first carriages the WC&P got hold of were originally built for the Argentine Republic Railway. They had a distinct 'American style' with open-end platforms and wrought-iron guard-rails. As railway historian Colin Maggs puts it, they were perfect for playing out imaginary westerns! After the railway closed, two ended up as school dormitories! Practically all the engines and rolling stock were second-hand, but one of the petrol railcars, bought in 1921 to the WC&P's own specifications, actually succeeded in hauling the company into profit for a short time.

Stories about the line entered local folklore. People loved the romance of drivers stopping the train at a favourite spot to gather mushrooms, to be taken back to Weston and fried up with bacon on a coal shovel. Apparently there were places you could lean out of a slow-moving carriage and pick blackberries! Accidents did happen; one at Worle in 1903, when a waggonette collided with the train, claimed two lives and left four seriously injured. Thankfully, that was extremely rare but cattle were vulnerable if they broke through boundary hedging and wandered onto the track.

During the 1930s, increasing road traffic took its toll on the line's already fragile finances and so, with the onset of war, The Excess Insurance Company called it a day on 18th May 1940. Little of the light railway exists today; a few broken bridge piers on the River Yeo and the trace of the line across various fields. In Weston, there is a memorial of a kind; part of the route through the town has become a cycle-way, complete with its own traffic lights at the top of Ashcombe Road.

(For much more on the WCPLR, read the accounts by Colin Maggs and Peter Strange - both listed in the Bibliography.)

Chapter Eight

YATTON

The south porch, St. Mary's Church

The B3133 peels northwards off the Weston/Bristol road a short distance from
where the main road bridges the River Yeo at Congresbury. From here, there's a
gentle rise as it ascends the western ridge of Cadbury Hill before descending,
gently, into Yatton. The village has changed tremendously since the war, with housing
estates expanding outwards from the High Street as farms and church buildings have
been lost to development. Thatch gave way to tiles and listed buildings (Court House
Farm) to shopping precincts. Fine period houses and their gardens do still occupy
portions of the street but the overall atmosphere of the road has been overwhelmed
by jarring infills and modern materials.

Mercifully, the area around the magnificent St. Mary's Church[67] has been well cared for. Its abbreviated spire is mostly invisible from the High Street, so approaching the building through an old iron gate and up a narrow, cottaged alley close to Church Road sustains a mood of watchful suspense. The tower looms large at the end of the lane, a lowering yew shades the high entrance gate, while

The Grey House, High Street

beyond, light pours onto the path that curves past the churchyard cross. The church is a building of great power, rising imperiously above the surrounding Northmarsh. There is a strong, vertical emphasis which draws attention to the beautiful, south porch adorned with the most delicate stone tracery. Each wall, the porch and tower included, is capped by a unifying and delicate, carved, stone frieze connecting the whole structure with the sky. All this harmony makes it difficult to understand the leaden aesthetics of the 1970s Chapter House on the church's north side.

There's a touching story associated with St. Mary's churchyard. Isaac Joules fell in love and married a beautiful gypsy girl called Merily. It has been said Isaac was disowned by his farming family for what they considered an unseemly union, although it appears he himself came from a gypsy dynasty, long established in the Yatton area. Isaac made a living as an itinerant knife and scissor sharpener - his grinding frame strapped to his back.

[67]*The former Norman church had a major reconstruction during the 15th century giving us today's wonderful, Perpendicular building. It seems the spire lost its top in 1595, after a hundred years or so, presumably because the tower and the foundations were not equal to the load - a familiar problem on the Levels. The porch was the gift of Lady Isobel Newton in memory of her husband Sir John, who died in 1488. Much of the money for the rebuilding came from local people who organised collections and events like 'Church Ales' in the nearby Church House. The ale, brewed especially for these occasions, was, I suspect, of superior strength - anyway a good time was had by all - including the church coffers!*

When Merily died in 1827; Isaac was grief-stricken, often spending entire nights by her graveside. His devotion continued until his own death 14 years later in the Axbridge Union Poorhouse when he was buried beside his beloved. On her gravestone is written:

Here lie Merily Joules

A beauty bright

That left Isaac Joules

Her hearts delight.

1827

There is a line of Romany graves, including the Joules family, north of the church, along the churchyard's east wall.

There was a time Yatton was a significant Great Western Railway junction with trains arriving and departing for Bristol, Weston, Clevedon, Wrington, Blagdon, Axbridge and Wells. Beeching put an end to all of that in the 1960s and, although the village still has a station (and some GWR benches), it's a shadow of its old bustling self. The main

Yatton railway station

buildings are still there (painted peculiar colours) and so is the footbridge - although it's lost its canopied roof. Much of the track of the old Strawberry Line, from Yatton to Cheddar and Wells, has been aquired by the Somerset councils and adapted into a walk and nature reserve.[68] It starts at Yatton station and is sonorously titled 'The Yatton Station Community Forest Gateway' which seemed a touch overegging to me.

[68] *When the line closed in 1965, local people took to using the old track as a walkway. An inspired group of enthusiasts, calling themselves The Cheddar Valley Railway Walk Society, convinced the various Somerset County Councils to buy the railway land while they, ie. the society, would help manage and maintain it. Part of the line has also been made into a cycleway, with the ambition that the whole route can eventually be shared by cyclists and walkers.*

Chapter Nine

KINGSTON SEYMOUR

The small road from the Kingston Bridge crosses the Rust Rhyne at the undistinguished Lampley Bow before it takes on the droning intrusion of the M5 motorway. So it was a great relief, once the motorway was behind us, to find the village setting still merited its reputation for isolation. It feels folded away. The roads here go to almost nowhere but themselves. They wander lazily beside rhynes and orchards to arrive back at their beginning; the axis of the village, a small triangular palisade containing a few trees, the village cross and a Somerset signpost. The signpost comes with directions to no place in particular other than whence you came - Ham Lane, Middle Lane, Back Lane and Yatton.

Gateway to
All Saints' Church

Ham Lane leads us to All Saints' Church; comfortably corralled behind high yews and a rhyne moat (until recently the rhyne completely encircled the church), with the track to the church making its way beside a low stone shed punctuated by the Post Office red of the village telephone box.[69] From the east gate, the path passes a medieval tomb-chest from the same period as the church (15th century Perpendicular) and made, it seems, from the same soft yellow-grey limestone. In winter sunlight, the steepled church appears warm and accessible with no pretence to the dominating elevations of St. Mary's in Yatton. There's a 600 year old churchyard cross here too, but in the porch is an extraordinary noticeboard describing the floodwaters that struck so much of Somerset in 1606 (or 1607?)[70] - and Kingston Seymour especially (see Special Page). In that flood, the water rose over the top of the church's pews and even filled the Norman font. This was at a time when the Northmarsh sea-defences had probably been neglected for some time. I had heard from somewhere that the flood level stain still 'came through' whenever the church was repainted - but we could see no evidence of that. Perhaps it was just rising damp! These are wet lands after all.

[69] *The telephone box is Sir Giles Scott's K6 design: the 1935 'Jubilee Kiosk'.*

[70] *Different sources: different dates...*

We leave the churchyard by the lychgate at its east end below the spire. Just beyond stands the former, splendid, Victorian school and in a lane close by, a sign for free-range eggs. The directions lead to Elm Cott and the eggs are neatly stacked for collection with instructions to leave a very small amount of money. As we turn to leave (with our eggs), we are greeted with a "Hello!" from across the garden. It's Franky Griffin,

and soon we are introduced to the hens and ducks that have laid our eggs, and are talking Kingston Seymour. It turns out her husband Roland and his family have farmed in the Kingston area for many years. Not only that, but Franky is a local geologist with an enthusiasm for the Somerset coast!

Molly and Roland at Mill Leaze

It isn't long before we meet Roland and all the family including Molly the dog. A week or two later we are being shown around. It's quintessential Levels; mainly pasture fenced by substantial rhynes - 'water fences' - as Roland puts it. They show us the drainage grypes (described in the 'Warth' chapter) and the abandoned lanes (now corridors of trees) that once crossed the farmland. The Little River runs through his fields; another of the water channels of some antiquity, draining into its big brother Yeo at a clyce called Phipp's Bridge, close to the motorway. The arrival of the M5, in the late 1960s, tore farms apart, with land separated on either side of the carriageways. Some fields were completely isolated; so a lot of unsatisfactory exchanges took place. Nobody was happy. There was compensation of sorts, although for the Griffin family it didn't come through for over seven years. Anyway, it could never make up for the sense of loss and violation - something I had felt myself when the same motorway pressed on south, through the serene Lox Yeo Valley below Crooks Peak.

Edmund Eglinton

Somerset Fisherman and Seafarer

When he got into his 80s, Edmund Eglinton, a Kingston Seymour man born and bred, was encouraged to write of his early experiences sailing and fishing in the Severn Estuary. He was born in 1902 and by the age of 16 had already crewed some of the trows and ketches that sailed off the north Somerset coast. Much of his early work was with his father Thomas, moving stone from Uphill and Clevedon to the sea-walls at Kingston and Wick. His book, 'The Last of the Sailing Coasters', opens with a vivid description of him and his sister Edith lighting a beacon fire, late at night, to guide his father's loaded boat ('a stump-masted, open trow') the *Providence* onto the mud-flats close to the Kingston walls:

"A sight never to be forgotten - a picture of a little ship sailing in and out of the darkness into the limited lighting of the flames of our beacon, seeming to float on liquid silver."

Edmund describes the desperately hard work of unloading the stone before the following tide and the ever present danger of the boat being wrecked by an on-shore wind. He continued work on the walls for some years, but increasingly became besotted by boats; the smell of Stockholm tar, oakum and pitch, the gleaming brass lamp in his father's cabin... He was eventually allowed to crew on the little trow *Jane*, bringing stone from Uphill. There was the occasion the *Jane* was struck by lightening just off Sand Point - his father, who had been watching from the shore, described; "The cloud seemed to curve down from the sky and cover you like a huge paw." On board, there had been a red ball of fire and a huge explosion, sparks falling about the ship, the smell of burning sulphur. The *Jane* was remarkably undamaged and after unloading the stone at Kingston Warth, Captain Smart headed north for Lydney on the rising tide. Edmund was impressed by two things on the *Jane*: Captain Smart's seamanship and the boat having a teapot as well as a kettle!

Continued

Master Eglinton was clearly a lad of prodigious energy. In 1917, with food scarce because of the war and while still working on the sea-walls, he decided to try his hand at stall fishing off the mouth of the River Yeo. With the advice of Mr Hayden, a Weston fisherman, he made his own 'tunnel nets', 6 ft square and 14 ft long - 6 nets in all. He knew about 'the gut', a channel in the mud formed by the scouring currents at the mouth of the Yeo. At low water on the spring tides, the gut dried out to a firm-floored channel which allowed you to 'walk up and over' the Langford Sands offshore. (You needed just a little local knowledge for this!) Anyway, Edmund then constructed a mud-sleigh (see the Stolford chapter in our West Somerset Coast) with a tallow candle to light his way. With the sleigh, he transported seven, 12 ft, larch poles and, at each low water, managed to drive two of them, 5 ft into the clay of the gut. Eventually, with the nets installed, he was catching a variety of fish as well as shrimp - cooking the latter in a copper stove he had erected on the shore and fired with driftwood. In the season he was able to earn about £3 a week - equivalent to the wages of three unskilled men!

He describes one extraordinary time when he arrived at the gut too early, on a very black November night. From the edge of the tide he could see a glow and, at first, thought it was the lantern of a boat - but there was no reply from his call. Alarmed, he watched the glow increase as the tide went out. Then, as he nervously approached the nets, he could see what it was - they were crammed with sprats shimmering with phosphorescence. It was the first time he had seen such luminosity in the muddy waters of the Severn Sea.

(Read the full story in: 'The last of the Sailing Coasters', Edmund Eglinton and 'A Young Fisherman in WW1' from Somerset and Dorset Notes and Queries)

At another time - a crisp, bright, February morning, with ice on the rhynes - Roland takes us to the small creek a short distance inland from the Yeo's mouth - it has a clyce (Mill Leaze Yere)[71] which controls waters from the Mill Leaze Rhyne. Walking along the embankment, we can see the sparkling mud flats of the river mouth peppered with a crowd of dunlin busy feeding. Taking our route inland, along the north embankment of the Yeo, we pass the old Weston, Clevedon & Portishead Light Railway jetty on the other side of the river - clearly ailing but remarkably intact - etched black in clear, winter sunlight. A way off, Wick St. Lawrence church and Worlebury Hill share the low horizon with the purpling haze of Crooks Peak and the Mendip Hills.

Across the Yeo, looking to Crooks Peak

[71] *Mill Leaze Yere; probably the site of a 12th century tidal mill -*
massive timbers were discovered here in 1983
(Local historian Keith S. Gardner). As to the icy rhynes, there was a time
(when we had real winters) you could skate over the frozen, flooded fields to Yatton.

The Great Flood of 1606 (or 1607)

Wonderful Overflowing of Waters in Summerset-shire 1607

The Somerset Levels, north and south, protected by their embankments and sea-walls,
lie several metres below the level of an average high tide - and even more so below the springs.
So, depending on the integrity of its sea-defences, flooding, at some time, was inevitable.
Indeed, some flooding was encouraged: the silt fertilising the land and the wet conditions
promoting the growth of luxuriant pasture. We were told that, provided the seawater ran off the
land fairly rapidly, a short period of heavy rainfall would wash out most of the residual salt.

It seems likely the Romans constructed the first sea-defences and after their departure in the
4th century, the Levels became flooded and were abandoned. Evidence for this lies in the the
thick layer of silt covering many of the excavated Roman landscapes. The 7th and 8th centuries
saw substantial reorganisation by the great estates and by the late Saxon period (10th century)
the Levels were effectively recolonised. Within a further hundred years, an organised and sea-
protected landscape had returned. Climate warming may have played a part in all this -
raising sea-levels and advancing the need for reclamation.

Continued

By the 14th century, the Levels, especially along the coast, were amongst the most productive in the region, generating considerable wealth and supported by an increasing demand for meat and milk. Nevertheless, organisation slipped during the 15th century and it was a failure of maintaining the sea-defences that may have contributed to the Great Flood of 1606.

However; the 1606 (or was it 1607?) flood seems to have been exceptional in its severity, extent and unexpectedness. Flood water stretched as far inland as Glastonbury and it's reckoned over 2000 people died in Somerset, Devon and South Wales. The waters reached their deepest in Kingston Seymour; as the notice-tablet in the church porch vividly describes:

January 20th 1606 and 4th of JAS 1. / An innundation of the Sea-water by /
overflowing and breaking down the / Sea banks; happened in this Parish /
of Kingstone-Seamore, and many / others adjoining; by reason where / -of, many Persons were drown'd /
and much Cattle, and Goods, / were lost: the water in the / Church was five feet high and /
the greatest part lay on the / ground about ten days

William Bower

With the advent of the devastating 2005 Indian Ocean tsunami, a more recent theory is that the 1606 devastation was caused by a tidal wave - a sort of gigantic Severn Bore. Research by Drs Simon Haslett and Tim Bryant of Bath Spa University suggests the wave was about 18 ft high and travelling at 32 mph when it collided with the Somerset coast. The wave could have been generated by an underwater landslide or earthquake in the Continental Shelf between Cornwall and Ireland - seismic activity is still registered in that area.

People in Kingston can still recall water coming in through their front doors and going out the back; 1981 was a time of particular anxiety - although it wasn't caused by a tsunami! Upgrading the sea-walls, better tidal sluices and cuts (like the Blind Yeo) has made the Northmarsh a much drier place - although no amount of improvement could cope with a tidal wave.

Not far from the jetty, we come to Tutshill Ear (yere), a large, modern sluice which controls the River Yeo's water outflow and it's here that any tidal flow upstream comes to a halt. With permission, it's possible, at this point, to cross the Yeo over a substantial bridge. On the south bank is a smaller clyce managing the water from the Oldbridge River; a straight cut draining the Puxton rhynes. The M5 is ever-present and where the Yeo passes under it, we are able to accompany the river along a railed walkway beneath the motorway. Phipp's Bridge is close by and it's a short way to the Roman Villa site from here. The morning ends with bowls of vegetable soup and Franky's freshly baked bread.

Apple orchard, Ham Lane

This area of Somerset was once famed for its orchards - Kingston Seymour, along with Congresbury, especially so. The trees were noted by J. Collinson when he travelled through Somerset in the late 1700s, and in the mid-19th century there were over 60 orchards, big and small, in the Kingston area.[72]

Local farmer Ken Stuckey's grandfather had a special interest in cider and amongst the memorable apples he grew were:

> *Egremont Russet - a small sharp apple, maggots loved 'em*
>
> *Sheep's nose - looked like its name*
>
> *Broad Leaf Jersey - green, difficult to find in the long grass*
>
> *Kingston Pippin - the Stuckey name for any apple they didn't like!*

A lot of tramps came by Kingston; it was the way they took between Weston and Clevedon. Ken's grandfather would put up a special barrel for the 'gentlemen of the road' - not too strong, it consisted, in equal parts of: good cider, poor quality and water.[73] Just to make sure, I suppose, they didn't come back for more - or be too tiddled to leave! There are still a few orchards and ancient apple trees to be found in Kingston, along Ham and Middle Lanes where they put on the finest blossom in May.

[72]*Ken Stuckey, 1982, Banwell Society of Archaeology Journal, no.18.*

[73]*Cider, whatever its quality, was rarely wasted. There was always someone who'd take a sup of it. Bill Wear, a farmer at Stonewell Farm, had 11 gallons of cider that was "Going off a bit." So he took it down the Dolemoors and left it. He soon discovered all the cider had gone and duly asked of his workers "What was it like?" The reply came; "Just right! Any better and we wouldn't have had it. Any worse and we couldn't have drunk it!" (from: 'Congresbury Pubs and Inns', Congresbury History Group 1985.) Note: 'Dolmoor' was woodland/pasture in the Puxton Parish area "doled out" for the use of local working families - see Knight's description in his 'The Seaboard of Mendip')*

Chapter Ten

HOOK'S EAR TO KENN AND CLEVEDON PILL

The separated sea-walls of the Kingston Warth come together at Kingston Pill -
an indentation in that sweep of coastline, south of Clevedon, which appears to have
no name. Offshore, but inside the sandbanks called the Langford Grounds, lies a
channel of deeper water known as the Langford Swatch.[74] The swatch gives access to
the Yeo and Woodspring Bay when the sandbanks would still be hazardous shallows,
and provides a shortcut for boats sailing between Clevedon and Sand Point. Kingston
Pill is a small, muddy creek which once received the waters of the Kenn River
(now much diverted) through the clyce known as Hook's Ear. The Kenn is yet another
laggardly stream of the Northmarsh but, wherever its waters go, there is still an
impressive roar to be heard from the metal decking, above the outfall at Hook's Ear.

[74]Swatch; a channel or passage of water lying between sandbanks, or between a sandbank and the shore. OED.

The section of sea-wall encircling the creek is of rather older construction, and there's a wide strand of saltmarsh littered with all the detritus of the Severn Sea: motor bike helmets, motor bike tyres, traffic cones (what's going on!), plastic bottles, plastic gloves and plastic seats, bleached driftwood, tree-stumps with knots of deranged roots flailing skyward and, dead camels (not really)… It's a shifty, soggy landscape, where the saltmarsh grass forms hummocks above a matrix of ooze. It's just so very untidy! But the curlews like it, and so do we.

Church Lane,
Kenn

A small distance inland and a mile or so north of Yatton lies Kenn village, separated from its coast by the motorway. It's a moorland place surrounded by rhynes, and roads that run as straight as railway tracks. Willows and ash, high oaks and sycamores line up along the field boundaries. Just off the Yatton road stands Kenn's curiously austere little church - its character lightened by a small, sandstone tower topped by a stepped, pyramid cap that might have been turned out of a mould like a blancmange. As we walk eastwards along the quiet Kenn Street, passing the church and the old school towards Yew Tree Farm, it's difficult to connect with the reality of Kenn being the scene of Somerset's last public hanging in 1830. We come on John Griffin at the church side-gate he's painting, he tells us the hanging ground is still there; a field towards the end of Kenn Street, opposite Moorgate House, at the junction with Duck Lane. We find it easily. It's an innocent place now, hedged and rhyned, a few cattle, overseen by some senior oaks and distant Clevedon's wooded hills. Yew Tree Farm is a handsome Georgian farmhouse and back in the 1800s it must have represented considerable wealth and power - it was a sequence of events connected with the farm that led to the execution of three local men. (See Special Page)

At its eastern end, Kenn Street strikes the Kennmoor Road at right angles. This is truly Levels land with the Kennmoor Road running straight and true for over two miles; from the wide 1950s drainage cut, the Blind Yeo, in the north, to Yatton in the south - the sense of distance emphasised by the progression of stately oaks and ashes along the road margins. The rising ground to Nailsea in the east and north marks the eastern boundary of the Northmarsh.

Back at the coast. From Kingston Pill, the sea-wall, mainly a grassed embankment, describes a shallow arc around Hook's Ear. The embankment continues alongside the shoreline saltings until it meets the concrete pavement that tops the wall, practically the whole way to Clevedon Pill. This section of the sea-defence is buttressed by large chunks of wave-breaking Mendip Carboniferous Limestone, and it's clear the sea repeatedly overtops the stone wall on the spring tides - as evidenced by the jetsam-strewn saltmarsh bank rising a further few feet above the shore.

Clevedon Pill

South of Hook's Ear, getting to the coast is somewhat circuitous, unless you ignore a notice or two and are prepared to negotiate a muck-coated embankment - you do get the feeling someone doesn't want you around! But access to the concrete pavement part of the wall can be made by public footpath from both Kingston Seymour and Clevedon and it's a popular place to run or take a stroll. Strolling north, Rosie and I watch the hump of Clevedon's Wain's Hill pull into view. The hill forms a small, grassy promontory, 37m high, nosing into the Channel. A sister hillock, known as Old Church Hill, rises to its north-east and in the cleavage nestles the 'old' Church of St. Andrew.

About a kilometre north of Hook's Ear, there's a moderate lift in the land on the seaward side of the path which goes by the name of Gullhouse Point. This grassy bluff is occupied by a few holes of the local Golf Club, but footpaths continue on both landward and seaward sides. Rounding the point, the path meets the substantial sluice gates controlling the outfall of the Blind Yeo[75] which, with houses pressed up against it, now forms Clevedon's southern boundary.

[75] *The Blind Yeo is a major drainage channel, cut in the 1950s, which receives water from the Nailsea and Tickenham Moors through the Middle Yeo and the Parish Brook. These days, much of the Kenn River ends up in the Blind Yeo too. To get an inkling of its complexity read 'Who Made the Land Yeo?' by Keith Gardner, 1998.*

In the lee of Wain's Hill

Crossing the Blind Yeo at the sluice gate bridge, the saltings of Clevedon Pill come into view. The pill itself is a small, mooring creek whose channel is fed by waters from the Blind Yeo together with the smaller Land Yeo[76] which emerges below Wain's Hill. From Gullhouse Point, the high footpath arcs around the saltings to meet the Land Yeo clyce at Wain's Hill. On the landward side, and substantially below the path, is a wide, sheltered field (a recreation ground called Marshall's Field) which, with its southerly aspect, is a delightful picnic spot. Indeed, standing on the sea-wall track, it's pretty clear much of this part of Clevedon must be below high water on a spring tide. The pill has a fair number of small craft moored on the mud-slopes of its creek. It also has its own sailing establishment: the Clevedon Sailing Club with a slipway and a high, stone-walled enclosure where dinghys are packed on their sterns, like biscuits in a box.

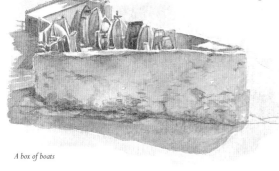

A box of boats

In the lee of Wain's Hill, Clevedon Pill is a peaceful, becoming place these days, but for much of the early part of the 20th century, it was a centre for the hard trade of ship-breaking. There's little sign of it now, and it's difficult to imagine the depressing clutter of dead and shattered ships which must have littered the haven. But a heavy, rusted windlass still stands above the Land Yeo clyce, a reminder of what Grahame Farr called 'a melancholy trade'.[77]

Windlass

[76]*The Land Yeo arrives in East Clevedon and passes along and under Old Street and Old Church Road before twisting its way, between the houses, to Wain's Hill.*

[77]*Maritime historian, Grahame Farr describes ships of well over 1000 tons being broken up: craft such as the Canadian full-rigged 'Thornhill' and the iron paddle steamer 'Velindre'. The hulks were dragged high out of the water on the spring tides by means of a windlass, well clear of the winter gales. One ship, an Aberdovey schooner, the 'Sarah Davies', caught fire after an especially dry summer - "... and she burnt down to her garboard strakes."*

The Hanging Field at Kenn

On a September day in 1830, the small village of Kenn was the setting for the last, public executions in Somerset. Three local men, William Wall, aged 35, and James Rowley and Richard Clarke both aged 19, had set fire to 'three mows of wheat' at Shortlands Field in Kenn. The wheat was the property of Benjamin Poole of Yew Tree Farm (some accounts say Laurel Farm) whose labourer Parsons had previously accused William Wall of selling cider without a licence and Wall had been fined £20. In those days, Kenn had become something of a cider fuelled rough-house of potato and sheep stealing; so this was clearly seen as an opportunity for an example to be set. The fated three were brought to the place of execution, Seven Acres Field on Kenn Street, where the gallows waited bearing the sign, 'For firing stacks'. They had travelled, sitting on their coffins in the gaol van, from the county gaol in Ilchester 40 miles away, to the 'Rose and Crown' inn (now the 'Drum and Monkey') on the Clevedon road. From there, and for the final few miles of their journey, they were accompanied by an extraordinary cavalcade: soldiers, special constables, the High Sheriff on horseback, magistrates, executioners… if there was going to be trouble, then it could be dealt with.

Kenn's St John's Church tolled a funeral knell. People had flocked in from far and wide - 10,000 was the estimate at the time! - "The elm trees were covered with people like so many crows!" - one tree branch gave way, tumbling its incumbents into a nearby rhyne. It had become what was grotesquely known as 'a Hang Fair Day'.

The condemned mounted the scaffold, accompanied by Rev. Valentine who asked them to kneel and pray. Final words were uttered, young Richard Clarke was heard to cry; "Cider has been the ruin of us all!" as they were pitched towards eternity. For Richard it was slow coming and the hangmen had to swing on his legs to finish their work. One of the crowd, years later, recalled a prayer-book slipping from a dead hand after a full quarter-hour. The bodies were made to hang for an hour before being cut down.

It's chilling indeed, at this remove, to consider three men's lives the reckoning for three stacks of wheat. John Griffin, who lives in Kenn, told me that William Wall's wife, Mary, was also implicated (William pleaded her innocence from the scaffold) but escaped the noose because she was pregnant. She was transported to Australia having given birth to a son David William, possibly in Ilchester gaol, after the executions. James Rowley's brother John was also transported. Since then, their distant descendants have returned to view the hanging field.

Accounts vary. This version of the story has several sources including Derek Lilly's in 'Clevedon Past' 1993. Farmer Benjamin Poole's 'three mows of wheat' were set fire in a field called 'Shortlands' - behind Moorgate House (where the Kenn poorhouse once stood), immediately opposite the execution scene.

Chapter Eleven

CLEVEDON - WAIN'S HILL TO SALTHOUSE BAY

South-west from Wain's Hill, low tide

The low, enclosing promontory of Wain's Hill[78] hides Clevedon from its small
harbour. From the Pill, the track runs below the hill, alongside the Land Yeo and the
western boundary of Marshall's Field, to meet Old Church Road: the way into the
main town. Before the start of the 19th century, Clevedon was a small and scattered
community, mainly rural in its economy with a diminutive fishing industry.[79] Farms
became established along the spring-lines below Hangstone Hill, south of which,
like the rest of the Northmarsh, the land was drained and divided by rhynes and dykes.
The 1839 Tithe map shows the 'Old Village' as centred in the area now known as East
Clevedon, close to the Lords of the Manor at Clevedon Court, but the true old village
was found around the Pill; a cluster of fishermen's cottages and hovels looking to
their Church of St. Andrew on the hill.

As we walk that way, on a spring-like March day, the road is warm and sheltered;
a natural haven, following a gentle, crooked course between boats parked up against
the side of the hill and the river, wooded slopes and allotments, a cemetery and a
sprinkle of thatched and tiled cottages. Admittedly, there's a good deal of the 20th
century about as well and although some of it masks the church from the road,
the ambience of a village street, somehow, remains. Along the southern side of
Old Church Hill are the vestiges of small quarries, hidden behind sheds and
woodland scrub, where Edmund Eglinton's father collected stone for the Kingston
Seymour walls.

[78]*Gabriel Wain was an 18th century landowner. In the 16th century, the hill and the pill
were owned by Margaret Pryston and entitled 'Prystons Freehold'. A Miss Priston married a
Mr Phelps and, for a time, the hill was called 'Phelps Hill'. The Prystons lived in West End Farm,
the larger of the two thatched farmhouses in Old Church Road (called Tennyson House since the 1930s)
and built in the 1500s (Jane Lilly and Clevedon Civic Society).*

[79]*In 1829, John Rutter considered Clevedon to be "more picturesque"
than Weston-super-Mare, although it did lack a sandy beach.
Its main deficiency, however, was "its want of a fishery".*

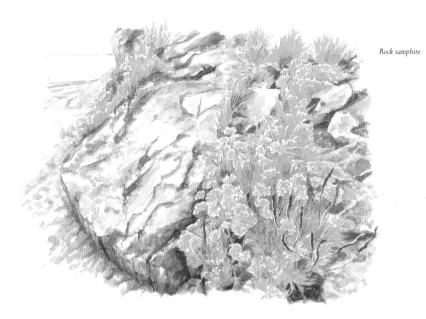

Close to the sailing club enclosure are steps leading up to the tip of the Wain's Hill promontory and a grassy shelf of derelict stone and brick buildings. These are the remains of the Clevedon Battery which had guns guarding the Bristol Channel during the latter part of the 19th century.[80] During summer, as on Sand Point and much of the rocky shoreline of north Somerset, rock samphire grows in unobserved abundance- here in the sun-baked crevices below the steps.

A few yards back from the Battery Cottages is the start of a path taking us over the promontory hills into Salthouse and Clevedon Bays. It rises and curls along the hillside edge revealing - it's low tide - a multitude of watery fissures making up the small, muddy delta of the Pill. The channel into the harbour is a sinuous trail defined by boundary sticks stuck in the mud - Peter Cumberlidge describes all this as; "a fascinating drying creek... marked, rather enigmatically, by perches". Offshore from Gullhouse Point lie the threatening, tar-dark Blackstone Rocks that guard the southern approaches to the harbour while to the north, below Wain's Hill, lie the equally threatening Spear Rocks. Local knowledge must be a useful commodity here!

[80]*Manned by the Somerset Artillery Volunteers and constructed in 1859. This was a part of the response to fears of French invasion which saw armed fortifications built on Brean Down, Steep and Flat Holm and Lavernock Point at around the same time. The battery practised on targets out in the bay. It was closed down in 1908. The first cottages you come to, along the track down from the pill, are called Battery Cottages: the residence of the battery Sergeant Major.*

At the summit of the hill stands a sunken World War II pill-box; an especially crude example of its type with small, unequal sight-holes and concrete steps down into its stinky interior. But from the pill-box roof we can watch out over the wide Severn Sea: thin, misted March sunlight, the flat, emerald green seaboard of Kingston Seymour with the blasted target-ships offshore; Woodspring Priory's tower at the eastern dip of St. Thomas's Head, Sand Point and wooded Worlebury Hill. Out in the Channel, Steep Holm and Flat Holm sit equidistant between the English and Welsh shorelines on a smooth, grey sea, with the west Somerset coast forming the edge of a barely defined horizon.

Wain's Hill, as with its sister promontories Sand Point, Worlebury and Brean Down, is a naturally defensible position and, like them, has evidence of Iron Age fortification - here, it amounts to the remains of a ditch and embankment which would have protected the fort's vulnerable (ie. no cliffs) western flank. The perimeter path curves down, following the dip between the two hills, with hawthorn hedges on both sides. St. Andrew's Church suddenly reveals itself through a thin woodland edge that looks down onto a well grazed field of donkeys. Before we see them, we hear a baleful, honking and hawing; more in keeping with the Greek islands - or the beach at Weston-super-Mare!

The church disappears for a while as the pathway runs below the churchyard fence and re-emerges as the track rises to meet Old Church Hill. Here the way separates into three: one continues along the coast and one takes steps (rather undermined by badgers) to the top of Church Hill. The third follows the line of the churchyard's stone boundary wall with St. Andrew's sheltered at the top of a shallow combe between the two hills.[81]

We arrive at a grassy plateau atop Old Church Hill and look down on the church with Wain's Hill rising to the west and the flash of sea and sky. Close to the steps is a sculpture of wooden uprights which, sadly, are rotting away at their bases. Of the original seven, only five staves remain, rendering the lines from Tennyson's 'In Memoriam', carved on them, rather meaningless.[82]

Following the direction of the encompassing churchyard wall, the path leads down to the main entrance of St. Andrew's; up steps and through a modern, wooden lychgate,[83] the church path passes by an intriguing array of chiding gravestones. It's a typical Norman (12th century) village church built of local sandstone in the shape of a cross with a central tower.

[81] Judging by old photographs, the graveyard has expanded remorselessly since the late 19th century, bursting beyond the confines of the original churchyard wall, to be constrained only by the hill's edge and the sea. It's understandably popular, but whereto next? The donkey field perhaps... The church lies two and one quarter miles from its manor house, Clevedon Court, in East Clevedon - supposedly the greatest distance from a manor house and the parish church in England! Until the road was built in the 1800s horseriders had to open five latched gates along the way.

[82] The lines from 'In Memoriam' on Michael Fairfax's sculpture should read:
'The darkened heart that beat no more;
They laid him by the pleasant shore,'

[83] R. S. Renton, who wrote the church guide in 1969, says "The gateway shows no sign of a Lich gate." A lich-gate (or lychgate) was the place the coffin (the 'lich' is the corpse) rested, usually on a stone slab, while awaiting the priest's arrival to lead the procession into the church. He adds: "As the available means of knowing the time were very crude it occasionally happened that the priest was late. This of course never happens nowadays." I wonder who he was having a dig at? Anyway, he was unsure of the recent fashion for "shelters over the gate"; which St. Andrew's now exhibits and sadly without a stone slab. Interestingly, the lychgate at All Saints' Church (1860) in East Clevedon comes complete with a coffin slab - though it's a tight squeeze.

St. Andrew's Church, summer, early evening

The upper part of the tower was added in the 17th century - we can see the change in the colour of the stone. Like similar churches along the coast (Uphill, Burnham-on-Sea), the tower was an important landmark for ships navigating the Bristol Channel and may well have been limewashed and furnished with fire beacons to increase its visibility by day and night. In the mid-19th century this church became a place of pilgrimage as a result of it being chosen as the burying ground of Arthur Hallam - the subject of Alfred Tennyson's famous monody.[84] Charles Harper, passing this way in 1909, hated the 'In Memoriam' poem (he wasn't too keen on Clevedon either) describing it thus; "To the healthily constituted mind, that verse is more than ordinarily revolting." But Arthur Salmon, writing a few years earlier, would have had none of that; he considered 'In Memoriam' to be one of the finest elegies in the English language.

Back at the coastal path, which through its literary associations has earned the title of Poet's Walk, the way continues above the quarried, north west cliffs of Old Church Hill and down into Clevedon Bay. Over the path's bramble and hawthorn hedge, Regency and Victorian Clevedon swing into view above a slanting, seaweed shore, the delicate pencil line of the pier drawn out from the blunt headland of Dial Hill. An hexagonal, stone-walled, lookout-point along the cliff path is the remains of a small keep from which the merchant Conrad Finzel watched for the arrival of his sugar ships from the West Indies.[85] The lookout was always small, but originally had a castellated roof and Gothic windows. A cosy place from which to watch your money arrive.

[84]*Arthur Hallam's death at the age of 22, in 1833, clearly affected Tennyson profoundly - they had met at Cambridge and became close friends. A marble tablet to Hallam is found in St. Andrew's south transept. Arthur Hallam's mother, Julia, was an Elton - the manorial family of Clevedon Court. An even sadder tablet records the deaths, in 1819, of two young Elton brothers, Abraham and Charles. Playing on Birnbeck Island near Weston, they became cut off by the rising tide. When they attempted to wade ashore, first the youngest and then the eldest was swept away. Francis Knight records that Colonel Oliver Rogers lost his life attempting to save them - he spent the day in a boat looking for the boys and died from exposure. According to Brian Walters, one of the boys' bodies was recovered from the Usk while the other was carried home by the tide to Clevedon.*

[85]*By spying the ships early and sailing out to them, Finzel was able to steal a lead on his competitors and negotiate an advantageous price. He lived for a while in the Salthouse, overlooking Clevedon Bay, during the 1840s.*

Poet's Walk

The way now folds back on itself, following the lower fringes of the sycamore woods that cloak the hill's northern slopes. It then runs above the margins of the open air Marine Lake, and down to the lawns below a handsome Regency building known as 'The Salthouse'.[86] From its woodland setting, its terraces look out over the Salthouse Fields (now the Beach Lawns) to a scalloped sweep of coastline subdivided into a number of pebble coves - Salthouse Bay, Little Harp Bay and finally Clevedon Bay.

[86]*The Salthouse started life as two cottages; the homes of 17th century salt panners who prepared salt by evaporating seawater in open pans behind the sea-wall - the wall was breached in places to allow this. The concentrated brine must have then been boiled down further to crystallise the salt. According to Jane Lilly, the salt was thrown against an upright sieve called a harp - this gave the name to Little Harp Bay. The Salthouse is now a restaurant and public house.*

Chapter Twelve

Marine Lake, Salthouse Bay

Since 1929, Salthouse Bay has been largely occupied by the open air Marine Lake. From the concrete walkway skirting its landward edge below the sea-wall, the Lake is like a vast infinity pool stretching out to sea. Sadly, it has seen better days and without its beach huts and diving boards looks uncared for and redundant. Maybe it's time for the old bay to return? The sea-wall here has a concave top that reflects the incoming waves; similar to the defences found in Burnham and Minehead and a reminder of how vulnerable this part of the coastline is to storm tides. On the promenade above is a dispiriting clutter of municipal seaside shacks bearing no relationship to the rest of the shoreline.

A little further north, the sea-wall merges into the rise above Little Harp Bay where the tilt of the rocks reaches the promenade to form a walled redoubt defending two windblasted trees. Expansive lawns (the Salthouse Fields) run away eastwards to meet Old Church and Elton Roads[87] which skirt the grounds of one of Clevedon's grandest houses - best known as Clevedon Hall[88] - built on moderately rising ground, its high roof, complete with a splendid belvedere tower, peeps above the treetops.

The Esplanade, Little Harp Bay

[87]*The Elton family, Lords of the Manor, secured much of the public open space for the town. Wain's and Church Hills, the layout of the promenade and The Beach, land for schools and churches were all donated by the Eltons. Arthur Elton shamed Clevedon into laying modern sewers through a Local Board of Health (1853) and he also helped found the Clevedon Cottage Hospital which opened in 1875.*

[88]*Conrad Finzel, the German sugar tycoon, built it and called the house Frankfurt Hall. A later owner, Charles Hill, renamed it Clevedon Hall. For many years it was home to St. Brandon's School for Girls.*

Many of the Victorian 'Italian Gothic' beach mansions along Elton Road have been lost in the past few decades. Houses such as Oaklands and Pembroke Court have been replaced with soulless modern blocks, and the vast sprawl of The Hawthorns, although better (from the front), really would be more in keeping within the confines of a gated estate on America's Long Island. Fortunately, enough of the original houses survive to ease the pain and Elton Road forms an impressive avenue as it curves away from the seafront and into the town. No. 5 Elton Road deserves to be 'a place of pilgrimage'; it was where important work in the development of penicillin and the discovery of cephalosporin was carried out during and after the Second World War. (See Special Page)

Back on the promenade above Little Harp Bay stands a charming, Victorian bandstand - a breezy place for a band, who must have found both their sheet music and their performances forever being blown away. A few yards further along, in an area known as the Green Beach, is a resplendent Gothic drinking fountain (and horse trough) which has earned itself a Grade II listing with English Heritage. It stands (since 1884), somewhat isolated, close to the road where it once supplied refreshment to both man and beast.[89] It just needs the water to be turned back on.

At the point where Elton Road turns into the town, close to the War Memorial column, Rosie and I take in the view that for many is the essence of Clevedon. It's a compressed perspective, with The Beach road dipping and then rising with a relaxed undulation. Pastelled Regency and Victorian villas stand facing the sea, most of them secure behind stone walled front gardens.[90]

[89] It's a complicated piece of masonry (sensitively restored by Clevedon Civic Society) consisting of: "a tapering, pyramidal top with foliage frieze, and pointed arches with crocketed gablets resting on coloured shafts, with crocketed capitals to each of the four sides". According to Andrew Hull, five types of stone are involved in its construction: Portland for the main body and red sandstone for the columns, polished red granite for the horse trough and drinking bowl, the lower dog bowl is polished white marble and the plinth York stone. The fading inscription once read; "A righteous Man Regardeth the Life of His Beast, But the Tender Mercies of the Wicked are Cruel"... which I don't entirely understand.

[90] One of these, no. 4, The Beach, is Waterloo House with an elegant arched doorway and classical proportions. It was given to the town by Victor Cox and developed as a Heritage Centre to tell the story of Clevedon. It's run by the Clevedon Pier Trust.

As the road rises, it meets the small copse and park on Alexandra Road[91] and loses itself between the Pier Toll House and Campbell's Landing Hotel at the entrance to Marine Parade, while to the rear looms a dark, evergreen canopy of Ilex oaks. Higher up the ascending hill line, runs the terracotta roof of the Friary Church and a mix of Victorian and 20th century houses cresting Dial Hill. Seaward, the promenade is something of a car lot, but it doesn't seem to matter, because the eye is irresistibly distracted by the alluring, defining symmetry of Clevedon Pier. (See Special Page)

[91] *This small copse and park is a remnant of the old woodland scrub that covered much of the hillside before the builders moved in.*

On the promenade itself, above the cliffs that separate Little Harp from Clevedon Bay, the tarmac path divides; one path running up to the Elton Road junction with The Beach, the lower passing below the shrubbery bluff that shelters the headquarters of Clevedon Sailing Club. One day when Rosie and I were there, the concrete jetty sloping down from the centre of The Beach esplanade was tricked out with the bright sails of a dozen or so sailing dinghys, waiting for the rising tide. They looked like so many exotic butterflies, wings open, basking in the sun. From the promenade, the pier reaches out into the sea in a sequence of eight low arches with graceful simplicity, and it stretches out to a pier-head pavilion of such delicacy, it would be perfectly at home on a willow-pattern plate. At low tide, the pier stands high and clear of the shoreline on cast-iron legs of seeming, and unnerving, fragility. When the sea is very high, say one of the equinoctial spring tides, the entire pier can look to be resting on the very surface of the water.

In October 1970, the two spans farthest out to sea, next to the pier-head, collapsed during safety tests. What followed became a roller-coaster ride for the Clevedon Pier Trust, formed to save it from demolition. An exercise in brinkmanship finally ended in success in 1989 when the restored pier causeway was reopened and the paddle steamer 'Waverley' was once again able to call - Rosie and I were aboard that boat on that sunny May evening. It was another nine years before the pier trust was able to position the refurbished, cast-iron pavilion and shelters back on the pier-head. But now we have it - Clevedon's exercise in perfection! (See Special Page)

The pier still has its castellated toll house (or piermaster's house) and wrought-iron gates which provide a touch of Scottish gravitas to the esplanade.[92] The house is now home to the Clevedon Pier Trust and includes a small artists' gallery. As well as selling tickets for the pier there's a good supply of nautical memorabilia and local books. In the 1980s, we had friends who lived in Ladye Bay (north Clevedon). From their living-room bay window, we could just see the melancholy, detached pier-head.

Pier-head shelter,
looking to Ladye Bay

[92] *The Clevedon Mercury of August 1868 wouldn't have agreed; it described the Toll House as reminding it, painfully, of "A sham castle, very like those chalk ornaments affixed to cakes." It was designed by Weston-super-Mare architect Hans Fowler Price who practised in an exuberant, eclectic style and wouldn't have taken much notice of the Mercury anyway! Less effervescent is his Royal Pier Hotel (built on top of Rock House: the original inn of 1822); fire damaged and in a parlous state at the time of writing.*

We would watch, late of a summer evening, as the pier would be mysteriously encircled by swirling clouds of roosting starlings, their flight synchronised by some extraordinary communion. Rosie and I visited the pier many times during its restoration - times both difficult and triumphant - so it's good now to be able to walk along the pier-deck casually looking for our names on one of the fund-raising planks. They'll be worn off by the time we find it.

Like all piers, Clevedon provides the experience of setting sail without leaving dry land - this includes that curious phenomenon of the land losing its familiarity when you're at sea. From the pier, Old Church and Wain's Hills look like islands with St Andrew's Church crouched between them - easy to understand from here the church's importance as a navigational landmark. The 19th century houses on Dial Hill, gabled and perched on the hillside, look fine, but along the sea cliffs of northern Clevedon, splendid villas have been sacrificed to late 20th century conglomerations of thudding tedium. They ignore the rise and fall of the headlands while, at the same time, from the landward side, they selfishly deny the passer-by any view of the sea.

'The Beach'

Villa, Copse Road

Once again, during the summer months, the paddle steamer *Waverley* and M.V. *Balmoral* make regular calls; offering excursions around the Holms, or to Penarth, Bristol or Ilfracombe. Perhaps, one day we will also see a restored pier at Weston-super-Mare's Birnbeck Island; then this part of the Somerset coast will be able to demonstrate a quite unique story of Victorian engineering and design.

Directly opposite the pier entrance, Alexandra Road makes a sharp rise away from The Beach. On the wall of the north pavement is a distinguished water fountain donated to the town in 1895 by Thomas Sheldon; again, like the Green Beach fountain, it's a shame water no longer flows.[93]

[93]*The fountain was a Doulton catalogue item and it would have cost around £10 in 1895 - you could have ordered one for your own front wall! That said, it appears to be the only surviving example in the country and it's now Grade II listed. When it was installed it was immediately popular, but the water stream was so slow "there were frequent relays of people waiting". (Andrew Hull, Clevedon Civic Society)*

Doulton fountain,
Aleaxandra Road

A short distance up Alexandra Road, a right turn takes us into Copse Road which runs parallel with The Beach and mimics its contour. It's packed with a mix of early and late 19th century houses and cottages, grassy pavements and street trees. On the east side of the road there is a terrace of engaging houses with Gothic bay windows, set back behind small front gardens. The road even has an excellent pub - The Royal Oak - and close by a tiled stall-riser (it reads 'PURVEYOR') marks the site of a departed butcher's shop.

The Saga of Clevedon Pier

Clevedon embraced the Victorian enthusiasm for piers in 1868, 21 years after its railway arrived. And its pier would turn out to have a strong railway connection itself; two London engineers, John William Grover and Richard Ward, came up with idea of recycling 'Barlow rails' - wrought-iron railway lines (designed by W.H. Barlow) previously used by Brunel's wide-gauge Great Western - by riveting them; either together to make piles or to curved iron pieces to form the arched sections. The pier needed to be light and strong, offering minimal resistance to wind and sea. It would have to cope with storms, a huge tidal range of nearly 49 ft and currents of over 5 mph. By extending 800 ft into the estuary, the pier-head would stand in 60 ft of water at high tide - sufficient depth for most of the channel steamers.

Continued

In their various configurations the rails were used to make up four-legged trestles linked by shallow arches. Each leg was attached to a 2 ft diameter cast-iron pile which was screwed down into the bedrock - until a 5 inch diameter rope parted under the strain of the capstans! On average, the piles went down 12 ft, although the longest descended to a depth of 76 ft. Each arched section was 100 ft in length, with each of the 8 arches taking anything from ten days to three months to complete - it all depended on the prevailing weather. At the 600 ft stage the pier was struck by a Great Storm but, very reassuringly, "not the slightest vibration was to be felt". The work was completed in 18 months by a team, on average, of 60 men: an extraordinary achievement. One man lost his life on the project; Henry Groves was dragged onto a windlass drum and crushed to death.

On Easter Monday, March 29th 1869, with the sun shining, the town bedecked and a public holiday, the pier opened to great celebration. William Grover, Hans Price and 100 guests sat down to dinner at the Rock Hotel while local children were each given 'a three-penny piece and a bun'. In the evening, the pier was lit up by eight arches of gas jets as well as fireworks and illuminations.

Continued

For some years the pier did well, but by 1890 the pier-head ironwork had deteriorated.
In 1893 the head was rebuilt using cast-iron and realigned with the direction of the sea currents.
In the summer of 1894 the pier-head was adorned with a pavilion and shelters
"in the Japanese style" - the complete pier had finally arrived.

The demanding environment of the pier exacted continuous wear and tear.
Local government had taken on responsibility for the pier in 1891 and for some time its care
was exemplary, but by the 1950s neglect was setting in. Every 2 years load bearing tests were
instituted - this involved flexible tanks pumped full of water to a load of 50 lb per square foot.
On October 16th 1970, the testing load was such that the 7th trestle moved, shifting the water
and increasing the strain. The trestle collapsed bringing down two 100 ft spans - the pier-head
and its pavilion became isolated and inaccessible.

Local government lacked the political will to act and, despite the formation
of the Clevedon Pier Trust and the pier's Grade II* listed status, applied for its demolition
in 1979 - this was refused following a Public Inquiry. Woodspring District Council then handed
over the pier to the trust on an extended lease. In 1985, the entire structure, save the pier-head,
was carefully dismantled, identified and shipped to Portishead Dock for restoration.
The collapsed 7th and 8th spans would have to be completely rebuilt.
Adversities continued; the original contractors went into liquidation, money had to be raised,
but on 27th May 1989 the pier, although still lacking its pavilion, reopened to local celebration
and once again boats were able to call.

It required another nine years of fund raising to see the Japanese pavilion and its
shelters back where they belonged, on the pier-head. On May 23rd 1998 the reopening
ceremony was performed by Sir Charles Elton, great-great-grandson of the first chairman of the
Clevedon Pier Company. Clevedon Pier is now regarded as a 'national jewel' and it
has a Grade I listing - but it so very nearly didn't survive.

For a full account consult 'Clevedon Pier' by Keith Mallory, and Austin Davis in 'Clevedon Past'

Chapter Thirteen

CLEVEDON - DIAL HILL

Hill Road

Dial Hill forms the apex of two ranges of hills that move away from Clevedon in
easterly and north-easterly directions, embracing the Gordano valley as they go.
Early in the 19th century, houses sprang up along the south facing slopes of Dial Hill
on land that had little agricultural value. This area of the hillside was sheltered and sun
warmed, and it came complete with glorious views. The building accompanied similar

developments along the coastline at The Beach and Wellington Terrace while parallel activity was going on in the 'Old Village' around East Clevedon. So, given its prestigious history, it's strange to stand in Hill Road today and find it full of shops. The grand houses are still there, but mostly lost behind an assortment of shop frontages. It seems that gradually, during the latter part of the 19th century, building on the hill's lower slopes meant the older establishments higher up lost their arcadian aspect. One by one the houses gave up much of their front garden to commercial premises. Clevedon was devouring itself, as arcadia gave way to trade. All the same, Hill Road still has a hint of what it was - Eldon Villas, high above the street, have beautiful terraced gardens that cascade down to the tall front wall - when we were there, it was draped in sweet alyssum. But despite becoming a different place, Hill Road remains an attractive, wide, sunny street with shops that are proper shops: ironmongers and hardware, a chemist and a baker, furnishings and clothes wisely holding onto their Victorian and Edwardian frontages.

Alexandra Gardens is a small, woodland park that falls away from Hill Road to Alexandra Road below. The lower road contains an especially exuberant building; the tiered pagoda of the Market Hall designed in 1869 by Weston-super-Mare's idiosyncratic architect, Hans Price.[94] Rosie and I love this building. After its splendid restoration a few years ago, it reopened in its original

The Market Hall

guise as a covered market. Sadly, that plan did not succeed as it had done a century before. But, at the time of writing, it's looking fit and well - as a health club.

[94]*The Market Hall came close to collapse during the 1970s but its quirky individuality saved it. When it first opened it was a true covered market with open stalls around its perimeter and even a fountain within. It provided selling space for small traders whose only option, before the Hall's construction, was to hawk from door to door.*

Discreetly hidden behind the most easterly shop on Hill Road's north pavement is the
'Zig Zag' path that makes its way uphill, behind the shops and houses. As we slowly
ascend, we get a glimpse of what those Bristol merchants were seeking when they built the
fine houses along the hillside below us. Although the foreground is filled with roofs and
houses, the tapestry of the coastline is unchanged: Salthouse Bay running into the wooded
slopes of Old Church Hill, a silver sea, the low headlands of St. Thomas's Head and Sand
Point, the high hump of Steep Holm down channel. A few cottages nestle into the hillside
along the way, but at the summit of our zigzag course stands Dial Hill House looking as
though it has just landed from Mars.[95] It's a remarkable Art Deco building, accompanied by
a magnificent Stone pine, standing high on Dial Hill, its great curved, conning-tower
windows gazing out to sea. Flat roofed, white-painted render, black line detailing and roof-
line decks; it evokes the North Atlantic passenger steamships of the Jazz Age.

[95]*Designed by architects Fry, Paterson & Jones, 28 Waterloo Street, Weston-super-Mare in 1934/35*
for Blanche Harwood, the stepmother of sculptor/businessman and local benefactor, Victor Cox.
When I first discovered the house in the early 1980s, there was still a small Deco gate onto the Zig Zag path.
The surmounting glass lookout is a later (post 1980), successful addition to the original design.

Instead of continuing past Dial Hill House onto Dial Hill Road, Rosie and I take the footpath (Friars' Path) west that leads along the hillside ridge, behind the houses and down towards the pier. The wonderful, southern panorama plays itself out from slightly different perspectives as the path descends, ending at a small grassy embankment next to the Friary church.[96] From here, the pier can be seen peeking out from behind the houses on Marine Drive.

From Dial Hill

[96] *Built in 1886, by a community of French Franciscan friars. They were replaced by an English order of Franciscans in the early 1900s. The friars acquired the former Royal Hotel which was knocked down in the 1980s for a new building, and the development of Friary Close.*

Across the road from Dial Hill House, a public footpath leads into the woods and grassland covering the crown of Dial Hill. We take the pathway north leading to wide, salubrious boulevards like The Avenue; tree-lined with pollarded limes, and from where roads such as Cambridge and Channel peel off steeply - down towards the Walton Cliffs and the sea. Moving south west, the woods open out onto an area of sloping grassland where a 'trig' point marks the summit of the hill. From an iron bench, we look out over the sequestered grounds of Clevedon Cricket Club.[97] The footpath leads us down and along the boundary of the ground. Walking past the practice-nets and the sight-screen frames; all that's missing is an Edwardian pavilion with a verandah. And it's such a beautiful setting! - the backdrop of the wooded hill topped by high pines, the gentle, green declivity of the pitch, an old horse chestnut marking the south gate. Memories of delightful games in summer sunshine.

[97]*Clevedon Cricket Club, founded in 1874, was soon playing regular fixtures with Weston-super-Mare. Being born and bred in the southern town, I have delight in recording one match against the club in 1881, when Weston's F. A. Leeston Smith Esq. scored 204 runs. Good man!*

Clevedon's Part in the Penicillin Story.

Early in the Second World War, the Vaccine Production Unit of the Royal Naval College Medical School decamped first to Barrow Gurney and then to the White House in Highdale Road, Clevedon. The unit, originally engaged in the production of typhoid and cholera vaccines, was now required to make an anti-tetanus vaccine and, because of this, was in contact with Dr Alexander Fleming (who had discovered penicillin) at St Mary's Hospital in London. There was a severe shortage of the antibiotic and production methods were pretty rudimentary - so the Navy decided to make its own. In due course, the Clevedon laboratory received its own supply of the 'Penicillium notatum' mould through its contact with Dr Fleming. The penicillin brew was likened to fermenting 'scrumpy' (cider), but trials on patients with chronic wounds at Barrow Hospital were spectacularly successful. This prompted the 1st Lord of the Admiralty A. V. Alexander (who was born in Weston-super-Mare) to press Prime Minister Winston Churchill to expand production.

Continued

Clevedon College at 5 Elton Road was closing down, so the Navy requisitioned the building and the Vaccination Unit moved house yet again. At first, practically any handy vessel (bedpans even) was enlisted to grow the floating mould - which was liable to sink if disturbed. In the end, milk bottles were found to be ideal and so incubator rooms packed with milk bottles in their thousands were set up. The atmosphere was sterile and maintained at 22°C, and the laboratory staff moved along the rows of culture bottles sitting on a 'bosun's chair' suspended from a massive steel beam. This was a uniquely Naval solution to the incubation problem!

5 Elton Road

At the end of the war the unit was taken over by the Distillers Company, but the demand for penicillin became so enormous the firm moved production to High Wycombe. In 1949 the Medical Research Council moved in and continued with the study and search for new antibiotics. In 1961 the Elton Road research station was closed down for good - at the very moment it had isolated the fungus Cephalosporium which had yielded a new antibiotic: cephalosporin. Cephalosporin was the first agent of what went on to become an invaluable family of potent antibiotics.

Information gleaned from articles by Michael Carlile and Roy Girling

Chapter Fourteen

CLEVEDON -
OLD CHURCH HILL TO CLEVEDON COURT

The Curzon Cinema

The distance between the parish church of St. Andrew on Old Church Hill and its manor house, Clevedon Court, in East Clevedon is nearly 3 miles - a long way for a time when such establishments were often next door to one another. The reason probably lies in the vulnerability of the Northmarsh to flood. During winter, much of the land south of Dial Hill could be underwater, with St. Andrew's isolated on hills that had become islands. Despite the few fishermen's dwellings about the pill, village Clevedon had not acquired a defined centre; farms and cottages were straggled along the line of what would become Old Church Road and Old Street. The route involved a fair number of gateways as well, all making the ride less than straightforward - not a comfortable prospect for the gentry attempting to attend winter evensong! However; in spite of the physical separation, the ties between the church and the manor house are close; they were probably worked upon by the same 14th century masons - their south porches especially, have many similarities. So, it seems the Lords of the Manor (the de Clevedons) elected to build The Court on drier ground, with secure roads to Bristol close at hand.

Sir Edmund Elton's clock, The Triangle

As I described earlier; the western end of Old Church Road, below St. Andrew's on the hill, still has the logic of a village street. But not for long. As soon as the road hits the junction with Elton Road it becomes a major conduit between the latter-day town and its seaside. It runs west/east, along the foot of Hangstone Hill, whose heavily quarried southern slopes rise precipitously behind the houses and cottages on the north side of the road. Amongst these, what is reputed to be 'Coleridge's Cottage' (see Special Page) stands with its semi-detached sibling (Coleridge's presumed homestead is on the right) almost totally obscured by front garden trees. There's no cosying up to the Romantic myth here! The traffic whistles by and a garage sits in Coleridge's scented bean-field directly opposite. Where's the Vale of Seclusion!? Whither "the stilly murmur of the distant sea"?

About a hundred yards further on into town, on the south side of the road, stands an equally remarkable building: the Curzon Cinema - reckoned to be "The oldest, purpose-built, continuously operated cinema in the World"![98] In 1920, the original 'Picture House' managed to keep projecting while the new, Art Deco establishment sprang up around it. A close look at the stonework of the west gable and you can see it's pitted and pockmarked. During the Second World War, a bomb exploded just outside the main entrance, killing a serviceman who just happened to be in the wrong place. A cruel irony, since his death was the only fatality suffered in Clevedon by direct enemy action throughout the war.

We now follow Old Church Road as it makes its way, through the Victorian working class part of the town, towards the Triangle, which has become the main shopping zone with a major supermarket and pedestrianised streets. This is where the Great Western Railway once terminated (immortalised in the road still bearing its name) and the Weston, Clevedon and Portishead Light Railway locomotives chuffed across Kenn Road. Roads from nearly all points of the compass intersect at the Triangle; a tight roundabout dominated by a handsome, wizard's hat clock-tower decorated with colourful ceramics.[99] Old Church Road now becomes Old Street, wending between closely built stone Victorian villas to East Clevedon and Clevedon Court.

[98] The Curzon opened as 'The Picture House' in 1912, built by Victor Cox whose father ran a Monumental Sculptor business in Old Church Road (now a post office with a wonderfully carved stone shop-front). The existing Art Deco building was constructed between 1920 and 1922, extending the original Picture House but all the while ensuring the performances kept rolling. The cinema's ornate stonework was fashioned at the Old Church Road yard - the pillars and huge 'Rising Sun' windows below the end gables. In 1945 a change of ownership led to a change of name; 'The Maxime' which continued until 1953 when the cinema was bought by the Cleve Cinema Company and the title 'The Curzon' adopted. In 1995 the cinema was taken into administration but was rescued by a 'Save the Curzon' action plan led by Jon Webber. The cinema is now a registered charity enjoying great local support and so continues to "continuously operate".

[99] The clock tower was designed and given to the town by Sir Edmund Elton in celebration of Queen Victoria's Jubilee in 1897. He made and fired the glazed ceramic tiles and panels at his Elton Ware workshop at Clevedon Court.

On the hill above, the slopes are covered in grand and enormous Gothic mansions built of grey-brown local stone. Many still have their fine porches and conservatories, attached and intact with graceful detailing in wood and glass. On the lower hillside, between Highdale Avenue and Highdale Road, a footpath runs past one of Clevedon's oldest buildings: Highdale Farm; a possible Domesday farm site.[100] It's set into the sheltered foot of the hill (much of which has, somehow, remained undeveloped); a cluster of farm buildings of different periods backing onto the grassy hillside. The footpath continues up the hill (bordered by drifts of cow parsley and green alkanet when we were here in May) to Highdale Road where we come on some of Clevedon's most graceful Regency houses.

[100]*According to Jane Lilly, its earlier name was 'Hidehall', where the estate's steward lived and administered the manor land (a hide is a variable unit of land). In 1297 the farm is mentioned as a chantry, probably serving as a 'chapel-of-ease' where the village could worship when St. Andrew's Church was difficult to get to - from then on it's mentioned in various transactions down the centuries. It is now a private house.*

Above the road, and gazing assuredly down, stands the very Victorian 'Mount Elton' - built in 1844 for the Dowager Lady Elton. In its time it was praised as being "A very elegant *cottage* in the new Tudor style." [101] A high footbridge links the house with the rest of its grounds on the south side of Highdale Road. Just below the house, the footpath enters the woodland that covers what is known as Strawberry Hill. Walking eastwards, we come to a track that looks out over the entrance to the beautiful Gordano Valley, with views all the way to the mouth of the River Avon and Somerset's northern limits. Across the valley stand the tree-covered slopes of Court Hill and below, on the valley floor, amidst the churchyard pines, the neat, Gothic prettiness of All Saints' Church. West of the church, at an angle to the Walton Road, is a cottage which has some claim to being where Coleridge and Sara stayed during their time in Clevedon (see Special Page).

All Saints' Church below Court Hill

[101] *Mount Elton's architect was Samuel Whitfield Daukes who also designed the Middlesex County Pauper Lunatic Asylum (later to become Friern Hospital) - I was a junior doctor there in the early 1970s!*
The hospital is now a collection of prestigious apartments.

Behind All Saints' Church, an iron kissing gate leads into Court Wood and the trail we choose climbs the southern slopes of Court Hill, some way above the terraces of Clevedon Court. The woodland trees are a mixture of beech, oak, ash, sycamore, holm oak and the occasional wych elm (much of the original larch and fir planting has gone) forming quite a dense canopy. Despite this, a persistent rumble from the motorway breaks through, becoming more intrusive the higher we climb. Our path winds up steps, through fissures in the rock, across a bridge next to a redundant quarry, finally reaching open grassland at the top of the hill - a carefully orchestrated progress.[102]

[102]*The wood was planted sometime after 1801 when enclosure allowed the Eltons to take over what had been mostly open common land. It was set out as a woodland park with paths excavated along the hillside, footbridges, rusticated stone benches and viewpoints to the Mendips and along the Gordano valley.*

Clevedon Court

Gaining Clevedon Court from the woods is not encouraged, and anyway it's best to arrive at the front of the house and be duly amazed. It's an extraordinary concatenation of buttressed porches and angled elevations stepped forward and back, windows of various shapes and proportions, gables and high chimneys.[103] We see it with spring sunlight on its muted yellow stone; softening, almost belying, the strength and authority of its medieval design. A huge plane tree stands guard at the gate, lawns stretch away to the west with horses in the fields beyond, and Christ Church tower picked out on the rising edge of trees on Hangstone Hill.

[103]The oldest part of the house (although opinion is shifting) is probably the fortified tower on the east side. With thick walls and slit windows, it could provide a defensible retreat in dangerous times; although there's no evidence it was ever needed. A smaller manor house was built in the mid-1200s and greatly enlarged in 1320 to include a first floor chapel (a hanging chapel) with a beautiful stone-tracery window - saving the gentry the long haul to St. Andrew's Church on the coast. Down the years, various modifications and additions were made, although the tremendous frontage has remained relatively intact. In the late 1950s, during extensive repairs, the unloved west wing of the house was demolished and in 1960 ownership passed to the National Trust.

Inside, the Court retains much of its medieval atmosphere; a 'screens passage', filled with arches and doorways, leads through the full depth of the house to the north side where the door opens onto the gardens and terraces below Court Hill. The hall of the original house (the Old Great Hall) now serves as a museum for the studio pottery ('Eltonware') created by Sir Edmund Elton between 1880 and 1920 and is now enthusiastically collected.[104]

The garden terraces and sloping lawns are wonderfully complementary to the house. Two high stone walls provide warmth and shelter to exotic shrubs and climbing plants. In late April, the crown of a great magnolia tree in full bloom stands out against the dark, Holm oak woods of Court Hill.

Magnolia in flower, Pretty Terrace

[104]*Edmund Elton was self taught and his creations are not to everyone's taste (including mine!). He used stylised floral and animal designs on shapes that harked back to medieval times, combined with vivid crackle and lustre glazes. Undoubtedly his greatest success is the Clevedon Triangle Clock Tower where he used a combination of glazed tiles and mosaics to satisfying effect. It should be noted here that Clevedon has a long history of pottery workshops which continues to this day.*

The Mystery of Coleridge's Cottage

Glen Cittage, Walton Road

Samuel Taylor Coleridge wrote some of England's most enduring poetry, and it was the short, happy time he and his new wife, Sara, lived in Clevedon, that saw the beginning of his most creative period. During the summer of 1795, Coleridge spent a lot of time energetically exploring the Mendips and northern Somerset, and it seems probable he was referring to Clevedon (in a poem to a friend) when he wrote; *'Up the rude romantic glen, Up the cliff and through the glade'*. In August, he and Sara decided to rent a cottage in Clevedon (for the grand sum of £5 a year) - which Coleridge described as 'The Valley of Seclusion' and certainly, in his time, the village must have seemed just that: a remote, bucolic idyll.

Coleridge and Sara Fricker were passionately in love and even breached the mores of the time by staying at the cottage together on August 20th - some 6 weeks before they were married.

> *My pensive Sara! thy soft cheek reclined*
> *Thus on my arm, most soothing sweet it is*
> *To sit beside our Cot, our Cot o'ergrown*
> *With white-flower'd Jasmin, and the broad-leav'd Myrtle...*

The Coleridges moved into the cottage in early October and recruited Samuel's publisher, Joseph Cottle, to supply them with domestic items such as: a riddle slice, one tin dust pan, a pair of slippers, 4 urine pots (!) Cottle even had the parlour wallpapered. The couple enjoyed an Indian summer on the coast, but by the end of the year Coleridge was fretting for literary friends and by early 1796 they were back in Bristol.

'Coleridge's Cottage', Old Church Road

These days, the problem with the cottage identified as Coleridge's 'dear Cot' is that it doesn't quite fit the bill. Joseph Cottle, in later years, recalled the cottage as being 'but one storey high' and this concurs with Coleridge's poetic *'Low was our pretty Cot: our tallest Rose / Peep'd at the chamber-window.'* The present, semidetached cottages are two storey (a plaque identifies the one on the right) and there is no evidence, from what can be easily seen, that an additional floor has been added. I suppose part of the problem is that the cottage is perched on Old Church Road - now one of Clevedon's busiest thoroughfares and light years away from Coleridge's secluded valley. It requires a real effort of the imagination to rewind to the late 18th century and experience:

> *How exquisite the scents*
> *Snatch'd from yon bean-field! and the world so hush'd!*
> *The stilly murmur of the distant Sea*
> *Tells us of silence.*

and, not unreasonably, there's a feeling the cottage should be nestling under Wain's Hill; where Coleridge walked and absorbed a landscape we can still recognise:

> *The Abbey and the wood,*
> *And cots, and hamlets, and faint city-spire;*
> *The Channel there, the Islands and white sails,*
> *Dim coasts, and cloud-like hills, and shoreless Ocean -*

Continued

For decades, the provenance of the Old Church Road cottage was generally accepted - although a few long-time residents begged to differ claiming "The poet lived in a little potting shed, in a garden, just below the old church - on the left as you go up from the road." In 1899, the Rev. Charles Marson (the son of a Clevedon vicar) wrote that Miss Frances Greville (whose father, Rev. E.C. Greville had known and visited Coleridge) was insistent the wrong house had been credited. She had always pointed to 'Glen Cottage' on the Walton Road in East Clevedon as the real one - "due east (sic) of All Saints Church and next door to the north of the blacksmith's shop. There are two cottages in this enclosure, and the poet's was the one next to the road". The cottages still stand (though now conjoined), due west of the church on the Walton Road, at the foot of Strawberry Hill.

Fourteen years went by before a Lady Elton rebuked this assertion. She stated that in Cottle's 'Reminiscences of Coleridge and Southey', the publisher described the cottage as lying in the village's 'western extremity' - not its centre. East Clevedon was barely a place at all! Also, a lithograph of the Old Church Road cottage, sold at a Clevedon Court bazaar in 1838, had been seen and approved by Sir Abraham Elton and his son Sir Arthur - both of whom "were well acquainted with the poet". Lady Elton was also convinced "Cottle would never have permitted a lithograph of the wrong house to be sold in Bristol during his lifetime without contradiction." Cottle died in 1850.

I suppose it's possible Coleridge and Sara actually stayed at both cottages:
one in August and the other from October.

So there you have it. But let's not jump to conclusions! I'm told there's a slate-roofed, single-storey, stone ruin under the hill at the quiet, extreme, western end of Old Church Road near the old church (I couldn't find it), although the consensus of informed opinion is that it was a pigsty. Not overwhelmingly romantic, but you never know...

The fragments quoted are from Coleridge's poems: 'The Eolian Harp' and 'Reflections on Having Left a Place of Retirement'. For a fuller story, read the evocative accounts by Berta Lawrence and Tom Mayberry. (Listed in the bibliography.) Charles Marson and Lady Elton's remarks are in Vol.45 (1899) and Vol.59 (1913), respectively, of the Proceedings of the Somersetshire Archaeological & Natural History Society. I'm especially grateful to Chris Richards for his help with this section.

Chapter Fifteen

THE GORDANO VALLEY

Walton in Gordano

Following the road north-east from Clevedon Pier and along Wellington Terrace, there's a mixed bag of buildings which, to a greater or lesser extent, hog the view of the sea - it's nearly a mile before Wellington Terrace gives way to Castle Road and the estuary is once again revealed. Fortunately, a short distance from the pier, at the top of Marine Parade, there's a cliff path (Lovers' Walk), its entrance guarded by a dark Holm oak, which travels above the shoreline below the high stone walls of private and hotel back gardens, to Ladye Bay.

During the 19th century, Clevedon expanded northwards to absorb the parish of Walton St. Mary - but not the village - for Walton (or more correctly Stoke-super-Mare) had already gone. At some time in the uncertain past, it decamped and moved downhill to become Walton in Gordano, leaving its church to fall apart above

Ladye Bay.[105] So the present St. Mary's Church (originally dedicated to St. Paul) was rebuilt in 1870 for the new families taking up residence in the Gothic mansions springing up all over Dial Hill and above Ladye Bay.

The beautiful Gordano Valley fills a sheltered space between the coastal high ground of Clevedon and Portishead, and the western extension of the Failand Ridge where it terminates at Tickenham and Dial Hills. So moving from what was a windblasted ridge, to just above the Gordano Valley[106] floor, must have made sense whatever the reason. The 'new' Walton sits in a sunny, south-east facing combe with its own spring-fed stream, close to the summer pasture of the Walton Moor. Today, much of the hillside between Walton St. Mary and Walton in Gordano is given over to golf. It's an impressive course with wide, dipping fairways and broad panoramas of the Severn Sea. High on the hill, close by, but virtually hidden by trees, stands Walton Castle[107] (best viewed from far below in Swiss Valley), once a romantic ruin for all to see.

[105] *Origins of the name 'Gordano' are all rather unconvincing: eg. it's a corruption of 'Gordenland' or derived from the Anglo-Saxon 'gore' a triangle or spearhead and 'dene' a valley. The latter does fit...just.*

[106] *This is something of a mystery. In 1791, Walton church was a ruin where, according to Collinson, "The traveller who visits this solitary domain is welcomed by no other sounds than the howling of the winds, the roaring of the sea, the lowing of the cattle and the bleating of the sheep..." Rutter considered 'Walton' derived from the Saxon meaning 'wild town'! The villagers may have left because church and thatched cottages were destroyed by pirate attack or despoliation by the Parliamentary army during the Civil War (the lord of the manor had been a Royalist), or it may have been on the whim of the lord to extend his hunting estate - but when this happened is unknown. The church was rebuilt in 1869/70 (architect: John Norton who designed Tyntesfield) incorporating what remained of the original church tower.*

[107] *Another Walton enigma. Possibly a folly, more possibly a hunting lodge, constructed in the form of a medieval fortress with an octagonal keep defended by a turreted outer wall. Built in the early 1600s by the Poulett family (Royalists who hit hard times for a while during the Civil War) it was apparently never completed or occupied. Charles Harper, passing by in 1909, considered it, in his usual, grouchy manner: "a flimsy and fast-decaying sham" - it being a mere three centuries old at the time! It was skilfully restored in the early 1980s and is now privately occupied.*

A public footpath traverses the golfing lawns, with golf ball impact health warnings to left and right, before it enters woodland (Rock Wood) that covers the hillside down to Walton in Gordano. A tunnel of beech trees opens out onto meadows shelving gently to the valley floor and lorded by conclaves of majestic limes. Rosie and I sit for a while on a wooden seat (placed there by Sir William Miles in memory of his wife Pamela) that looks out over a beatific Somerset landscape of grassland, orchards and woods. A short distance on and the path closes at the small churchyard of St. Paul's - a modest, enlarged chapel of red sandstone.[108]

Walton Street

[108] *Modest it may be, but charming none the less - its scale fits the village perfectly and there's an unusual defensive ha-ha.*
Inside is a small Henry Willis organ squeezed to one side of a tiny chancel whose ceiling is painted a dramatic green.

With the expansion of Portishead, the narrow road through Walton in Gordano has become something of a rat-run with a formidable press of traffic. Somehow, the village manages to ignore the cars; many of the cottages are side-on to the street while the stream, rising on the hillside above, burbles away contentedly to itself beside the road. A couple of miles along and straddling the busy Clevedon to Portishead road (B 3124) is Weston in Gordano. Modern traffic flow has disrupted its 'villageness' but, in the recent past, this must have been a semi-industrial place, with the working quarries on the hill serviced by the Weston, Clevedon and Portishead Light Railway tracking across the moorland below. We make our way through the hayfields to Valley Road which cuts north from the main road dividing the Black Rock Quarry as it goes. There's an old lime kiln here - set back off the road. The quarry presents steep faces of Carboniferous Limestone rising sheer from a flat quarry floor.[109] Above the quarry stretches Weston Big Wood; 92 acres of woodland, some ancient with rare sections of Small-leaf lime[110] coppiced from the time of Domesday. There has probably been woodland here for some 10,000 years, since the retreat of the last Ice Age.

A footpath, opposite the wood, leads us over the hill to the ruins of Manor Farm; abandoned in the 1950s when the quarry hoped to munch up more of Somerset. The farmhouse and the old barn stand at right angles to one another, their gable ends still largely intact but their main, stone walls fast falling apart. The wreckage of a beautiful farm, its driveway still clearly seen crossing the fields, epitomises the vulnerability of this fragile landscape - something evinced by the houses of Greater Portishead, already visible, marching up over the hill.

[109]*Chris Richards of the North Somerset Museum worked there for several years during the 1980s -*
"I was responsible for a lot of that; blasting away great slabs of rock."

[110]*The Small-leaf lime (Tilia cordata) is an indicator tree of ancient*
woodland and surviving stands are rare in Great Britain.
Its relation, the Broadleaf lime (Tilia platyphyllos) is the only other native lime,
although the two have got together to form the hybrid Common lime (Tilia x europaea)
which was often planted in parks and streets.

Leaving the old farm, the footpath takes us back to the south facing slopes, meeting up with an old bridleway sharp with the smell of hawthorn blossom and nettles. From the hill slope, we can look across the Gordano valley to where the M5 motorway, slashed into the side of Tickenham Hill, emitted an ineluctable din of never-ending traffic but which, thankfully, quietens a little as we descend to Weston village. The Church of St. Peter and St. Paul, which somehow managed to side-step Victorian 'improvement', deserves its Grade I listing.[111] It's a red sandstone building of unadorned simplicity; from its small, "unbuttressed" tower to the peaceful solemnity of its interior. Mind you, it is a surprise to discover the altar's Eltonware legs when the altar cloth was discreetly raised - definitely not medieval; they look like a row of ceramic capacitors from an electrical relay station!

[111] *The church was built by the De Perceval family who crossed to England with William the Conqueror.*
Richard Perceval accompanied Richard I on his 1190 Crusade,
where he succeeded in getting an arm and a leg chopped off.
He's supposed to be buried (well, most of him) in the tomb close to the porch.
The village cross was erected in 1912 in memory of Spencer Perceval who, in 1812,
managed to be the only British Prime Minister to get himself assassinated.
Stones from the original cross form the base of the village pump on the main road.

A small, Gothic, iron gate at the back of the churchyard leads down to a field planted with young trees and to the old trackway of the long departed Light Railway, now part-incorporated into the Gordano Valley Nature Reserve as a series of 'permitted paths'. It's a delight to come across 'Mason's Orchard' (in memory of Laurie Mason 1905 - 1999) planted with cider apple trees: Redstreak and Hangy Down - all in blossom and doing fine.

The Gordano Valley from
St. Peter and St. Pauls Church

A number of droves[112] traverse the valley, roughly north/south, linking the two roads (the B3124 to the north and Clevedon Lane in the south) that skirt the moorland some 15m above its floor. Up above Clevedon Lane runs 'The Great Intruder': the M5 motorway and its pernicious drone, which we have to accept and put to one side - and just get on with enjoying this beautiful place. Clevedon Lane huddles along under the hill and ends at The

Black Horse Inn[113] in Clapton in Gordano. From here we walk under the motorway and through the woods to the crest of Tickenham Hill and then along the lane to Cadbury Camp.

[112]*Formerly wide, grassy tracks along which cattle were driven. Could extend many miles.*

[113]*A legacy of the area's coal mining days - there are numerous old workings and capped mines in the fields nearby. Folklore has it that the horses were black with coal-dust.*

After the bosky enclosure of the lane, the camp reveals itself as a wide, open meadow encircled by grassed-over ditches and walls; a familiar pattern of Iron Age encampment on Somerset hillcrests and peninsulas.[114] The hill-fort covers an area of about 6 acres and has spectacular views over Kingston Seymour to St. Thomas's Head and Middle Hope in the south and (between the trees) to the Second Severn Crossing and the Severn Bridge in the north.

South from Cadbury Camp

From the camp, a footpath takes us down through the woods towards the motorway, which we cross over a narrow footbridge while cars hurl themselves at dizzying speeds below us. On the north side of the bridge, the woodland scree is covered by a tracery of wild strawberries, dog violets, grasses and bright sun spurge. To the south, the bridge dives into a Sweet chestnut wood whose floor has succumbed to a haze of bluebells.

[114]*The hill-fort was probably constructed by the Dobunni tribe, whose range stretched from Gloucestershire to much of Somerset, around 300 BC. Unlike another important, Dobunni hill-fort on Worlebury Hill in Weston-super-Mare which had massive dry-stone fortifications, Cadbury Camp had lower walls topped by a high wooden palisade. Although the camp's features are predominantly Late Iron Age, the discovery of a bronze spear indicates that the hill was occupied some 1000 years earlier. The camp was also a likely site for a Roman temple; a small stone Roman altar statue, depicting Mars the god of war, was found here. The term 'Cadbury' derives from 'Cada': an early Anglo-Saxon name and 'bury': a fortification.*

Crossing the fields back to the village, we arrive outside Clapton Court, standing against the hillside, its parish church of St. Michael, just visible on a woody bluff, close by.[115] In the churchyard, by the path, is a censorious group of gravestones, heavy with advice and not a little spooky:

A.H.

Farewel my Wife, and Children dear.

I am not dead but sleeping here

My debt is paid, my Grave you see.

Prepare yourselves, and come to me.

I should have thought the "and come to me" bit would have had 'Wife and Children dear' taking off, briskly, down the hill!

The footpath leads from the churchyard gate (stone steps over the wall should you prefer), across hillside fields, back to Clapton, where we discover the Woodland Trust has been busy - they've planted 'Tynings Wood' on gently sloping land, looking west across the Gordano Valley to Weston Big Wood and its ancient woodland of Small-leaf limes.

Clapton Court

[115]*Church and manor house are built from the same rusted sandstone.*
The house is a meld of different periods unified by the medieval, west facing porch-tower with an arched doorway.
St. Michael's Church is Grade I listed and retains 'many Norman features despite a lot of Perpendicular alterations'.

Chapter Sixteen

LADYE BAY TO BLACK NORE POINT

Ladye Bay

Rosie and I have an affectionate familiarity with Ladye Bay. We have close friends who once lived there - in a gigantic, Victorian house (Upton Cottage!) overlooking the sea. It was in the late 1970s and Clevedon Pier was still disconnected from its pier-head - we could just see it from Upton Cottage's bay windows - sad, but at that time becoming emblematic of a new, positive perception of Victorian engineering and design. On a winter's night the wind would blow straight in from the Channel. The glass in the windows flexed with the gale force and the candles on the dining table would gutter. In summer, the windows would be thrown open and in the late evening we could watch the sun setting and mimicking the colour of the wine in our glasses. Whatever the season, it was one of the very best places to be.

On Guy Fawkes Night our friends would organise a bonfire party on the beach with hot soup, sausages and cheese and Marmite whirls. Our young son Sam held Susan's hand by the sausages, while daughter Katie helped Andy with the Chinese ordnance: Hong Kong howitzers, Peking fusillades, screaming air missiles - he usually finished off with multiple explosions of such brain crushing concussion our ears rang for days, and Sam hid further behind Sue and the sausages.

Twenty five years later, Rosie and I are back in Ladye Bay with Franky Griffin, a local geologist. The steps down to the beach have been rebuilt and the rusty handrail replaced, which is a pity because they part-obscure what we have come to see - the striking, geological fault-line which divides the bay's cliff face. Looking back at the cliff we can see that the face is divided, left and right (ie north-east/south-west), by a fissure with rocks of different geological periods on either side. Conveniently, the rocks have quite different colours: to the left is Old Red Sandstone with strata of rusty red and dull sand, to the right is Triassic sandstone, a more definitive yellow. Equally striking is the difference in the angles of the rock strata: the Triassic sandstone leans back, away from the beach, giving a definitive shape to the cliffs stretching away towards the distant pier, whereas the Old Red Sandstone leans forwards. The reason the beach exists is because the fault has given the sea an opportunity to exploit a line of weakness.

Pebbles from Ladye Bay

We climb north-east out of Ladye Bay and along the coastal path, closed over at first by a canopy of hawthorn and sycamore. Emerging from the trees, we recognise a path we had descended in the spring which follows a steep ascent towards Walton Castle. Not far up, we had come upon an area of cleared woodland covered with bluebells of a particular colour (an intense ultramarine-violet) which we had noticed before in bluebells growing on the cliff tops between Minehead and Porlock in west Somerset.

Below the coast path, the shoreline changes its appearance: curious horizontal pavements stand clear of the sea, pocked and lumpy, sprouting clumps of grey-green marine grass. Closer inspection reveals they consist of rocks and pebbles of varying size bound together in a sandy cement. These are raised beaches of Triassic conglomerate sitting on top of the Devonian Old Red Sandstone. Walking along these pavements, Franky points out a small area which she describes as "a ripple pool". It looks like the corrugations left in the sand when the tide goes out. Which is just what it is except the tide has gone out some 250 million years ago! Apparently, from some of these impressions it's possible to determine the direction and strength of the Triassic wind and even if it was raining! A fossilised moment in time.

Franky and an unconformity

Margaret's Bay

A little further along, at Margaret's Bay, erosion and collapse makes it possible to see the lumpy Triassic conglomerate sitting directly on top of the Old Red Sandstone, like crudely poured concrete.[116] Not far away, Franky shows us a fault-line where adjacent rocks had moved against one another leaving a trail of crushed stone; she calls this "slicken sides".

[116]*The Devonian Old Red Sandstones were laid down 360 - 410 million years ago; some 150 million*
years before the Triassic conglomerate rock. Geologist Peter Hardy points out that the intervening
Carboniferous and Permian periods (360 - 250 million years ago) are missing!
During that time the Carboniferous rocks had formed - only to be eroded away by the time the Triassic
came along. This is known as an 'unconformity'. The Carboniferous is present on the other side
of the coastal ridge (the limestone of Black Rock Quarry) and up the coast at Battery Point.

The coast path winds on, a yard or two back from the cliff edge, bordered by bracken and the cheerful spikes of Rosebay willow herb. With the tide out, the shoreline is etched and scalloped into a fretwork of pools and gold sand. Speckled Wood and Gatekeeper butterflies dance ahead of us along the path - never quite resting long enough for us to take a close look at them. At Culver Cliff the route rises quite steeply and some way above stands the white tower of the Walton Bay Signal Station with its rotating radar aerial.[117] A few steps up from the track is a perfectly positioned bench upon which, unlike the Speckled Wood butterflies, we take a rest and enjoy the westering sun.

Shoreline below Coastal Path, low tide

[117] *The signal station stands some 43m (141 ft) above sea-level. It was used to signal ships that "all was ready"*
for them to continue to the Avonmouth, Portishead or Bristol docks. Many would be waiting at 'passage anchor'
in Walton and Charlcombe Bays for the tide and their turn in the queue. The signalling was originally through flags
hoisted on the station's flagstaff, but later Morse code signals by flashing light took over, with a landline to the Haven
Master's office at Avonmouth. These days technology has moved on; the station is unmanned and in recent years its
flashing position light has been extinguished but it still bears its rotating radar aerial. Oddly, when Grahame Farr
passed by in 1954, the tower was painted black - presumably a hangover from the war.

The Old Signal Station, Walton Bay

The path then follows the cliff-line a fair distance above the sea. In places there are deep, erosional gulleys where the pathway has become vulnerable and wooden walkways are needed. Tree-tunnels of wild damson, hawthorn and ash are scented with clambering wild clematis, bramble and honeysuckle. They hide the sea, almost completely at times. At Walton Bay, where mobile-homes press close to the shore, there's a cove with a few rough steps cut into the rock face and the remains of a rusting handrail to let us down onto the beach. A small stream squeezes out from between the strata nearby, cutting a groove in the rock before giving itself up to the pebbles and the sea.

For a while, the way returns to a mix of grassland and heath, and for us it seems to breathe more freely. Once more there's a clear view of the sea and the coastline curves comfortably to Charlcombe Bay where a narrow, woody combe runs back from the sea. The path slides easily into a small, scruffy cove, chock-full of jetsam and bleached logs - a summer holiday haven of sea-junk. Back on the cliff top, the path circuits a meadow of summer grass before becoming corralled by the high wire netting and lumpy earthworks of 'Babcock's Infrastructure Services'. For a short distance, we find ourselves in suburban Portishead walking alongside Hillside Road which runs close to the low cliffs - indeed, it eventually turns out that houses now occupy much of the coastal hillside from hereon.

Approaching Black Nore Point

Despite that, the National Trust has managed to secure a small patch of coastal woodland above Redcliff Bay where the path widens and the sea appears to retreat. It's a curious mix of trees: oak and field maple, then a collection of beeches above a sequence of small coves. A short distance beyond here, we catch our first glimpse of the Black Nore Point Lighthouse peeking out from beyond the trees. And then, emerging from the woods, we are there - a pebble beach and flat, red rocks shelving to the low, Black Nore promontory across a wide and shallow bay. The lighthouse strikes a splendid pose - an immaculate whiteness against a blue sky and high clouds. Powerfully built on its rocky platform,

The Nautical School Tower

with six, iron legs and riveted like a Dreadnought; it bears testimony to the quality of Victorian engineering.[118] Equally impressive, on the hillside above, stands the imposing, towered building that once housed the National Nautical School (see Special Page) which rescued many destitute boys and educated them for a life in the Royal and Merchant Navies. On the very crest of the hill above us, up until 1978, there once rose the tall, aerial masts of the Portishead Maritime Radio. For 50 years this small Somerset town was a major player in marine communications as well as naval education.[119]

[118]*The lighthouse was established in 1894 and the Ashford family of Nore Farm*
were its keepers from then until 1979, when Jim Ashford retired!
Up to 1940, the lamp was gas operated with a storage tank supplied from the village mains,
it had to be lit and extinguished twice a day with weights driving the revolving optics.
The light was converted to electricity in 1940, but with a master switch at Nore Farm for blackout during an air raid.
The lighthouse was fully automated in 1970. The height of the tower is 11 metres and the light 11 metres above
mean high-water. The light is white, flashing twice every 10 seconds with an intensity of 12,000 candela.
It's visible for 15 miles. (Trinity House, Sandy Tebbutt and Ken Crowhurst)

[119]*"A friendly voice on many a dark night."*
In 1919 the General Post Office and the Marconi Wireless Telegraphy Company
opened a long-distance radio station at Devizes with a guaranteed range of 1,500 miles.
In 1928 the operation moved to Somerset and the Portishead Maritime Radio
(with transmitters at Portishead and Highbridge) was born.
It initially served commercial needs, expanding rapidly during the 1930s
with heavy use by transatlantic liners and aircraft (flying boats etc) all using radiotelegraphy (morse code).
During World War II the Navy also became involved. After the war, commercial services continued to expand,
with a number of sites around the country all going under the name 'Portishead Radio'.
By 1974 the station employed 154 radio officers.
Gradually computer based handling systems were introduced
resulting in the closure of the Portishead station in 1978.
However, the famous name 'Portishead Radio' lived on until April 30th 2000,
when it closed after 81 years of service. In the end, satellite communication rendered
the Morse telegraphy and radiotelephony redundant. (Larry Bennett)

We sit below the lighthouse with the merest slip of a rising tide. The coastline towards Portishead is hidden from view, but Wales is ever closer. Looking south-west, Hung Rock and Culver Cliff block out Clevedon, leaving Sand Point and Steep Holm to demarcate the southern horizon.

The lighthouse at Black Nore Point

H.M.S. *Formidable* and the National Nautical School

During the 1860s, Henry Fedden, a Bristol businessman, was determined to rescue the 'Homeless and Destitute Boys' of his city's streets. So he leased a redundant wooden warship from the Admiralty to provide accommodation for a nautical school. The warship was HMS *Formidable,* a 2,289 ton two decker 'pierced' for 84 guns, built at Chatham in 1825. She had seen largely uneventful service in the Mediterranean and by the late 1860s lay at anchor at The Nore (another one!) in Sheerness. *Formidable* was towed to Portishead in 1869 and moored a short distance off the Portishead Pill in sheltered water known as the King Road.

Over the next 40 years more than 3,500 boys were trained at the nautical school in general studies, seamanship and trades, starting at around the age of 10 and leaving at 16. The finer arts of sailing were gained on a much smaller ship, a graceful brigantine called the *Polly,* moored in attendance close by. Most boys went on to enter the Royal or the Merchant Navy - many of the Bristol Channel pilots were *Formidable* old boys.

Continued

By 1899 the old ship was in a bad way; copper sheathing had perished and oakum in the seams was rotten A steam tug *Iris* had to stand by for emergencies! A severe storm in 1900 shook up the ship badly and it was decided what was needed was a land-based school. Architect Edward Gabriel was commissioned and the foundation stone was laid, during the summer of 1904, on the hillside above Black Nore Point. The boys moved into the new school in January 1906. It was (and is) a splendid building, "styled in the Edwardian Baroque" with an arched terrace, cupolas at both ends of the two wings and a magnificent central clock tower topped by a two storey lantern. A dynamic expression of self-confidence and power.

Edward Gabriel's building served for 76 years, closing to its last boys in 1982. For a while, it looked as though the building would be lost, but wise counsel prevailed and it has been converted into an apartment complex, named after Henry Fedden who started the whole thing off.

Sources: articles by 'Miss Worboise' and Bryan Little

Addendum: Rosie's maternal grandfather, Thomas Gosling, trained on *Formidable* from 1891 to 1895 and his very creased training certificate survives. There's a family story he later crewed for the Bristol Channel pilot boats. On 26th November 1916 while serving in the Royal Naval Reserve, his ship, the drifter HMD *Michaelmas Daisy,* was struck by an enemy mine "during a gale of wind and a nasty sea" and was lost.

Training Ship "Formidable"

LYING OFF PORTISHEAD.

Chapter Seventeen

PORTISHEAD
SUGAR LOAF BEACH TO BATTERY POINT

Nore Park Cottage

From Black Nore Point the cliff-path continues to skirt the housing estates that have sprung up on the northern slopes of Portishead's West Hill. Access to this part of the coast has subsequently become rather problematic; the old footpaths become lost between the houses and are not always clearly signed - it's easy to get lost as the roads branch off, and then branch yet again. The way seems to have become a secret few people want to share!

Leaving the lighthouse, Rosie and I continue, north-east, around the small promontory. The path is only two to three metres above the high tide mark and the coast is made up of a sequence of small, pebbled bays. Almost immediately, we arrive at a cove where Nore Park Cottage[120] stands on a rocky bluff, its footings protected by what looks like boulders of Mendip limestone.

Erosion is clearly a problem here, and where the cliff-path has been undermined it's shored up with unsightly brick. The low cliff-face continues with crags of Old Red Sandstone topped by the pudding-like Triassic conglomerate, as described in the previous chapter. The rock-face has a worn-out appearance and great chunks of conglomerate have broken away and lie scattered on the beach, where easily eroded sandstone is washed away beneath it.

Sugar Loaf Beach

[120]*According to local historian Sandy Tebbutt, Nore Park Cottage was built in 1870 for the gardener of Nore Park, a house further up the hillside.*

From Nore Park Cottage the path rises and is shaded by hawthorns and high pines. Walking here in early June, various perennial geraniums are flowering along the way, escapes, presumably, from the gardens the path squeezes past. The track now dips down into Sugar Loaf Beach[121] where the Portishead Lifeboat Trust[122] and The Portishead Yacht and Sailing Club share a concrete slipway to the sea. The lifeboat is stored in a modest boathouse, with a green-painted lockup raised above the beach. Across the slipway stands the brick Yacht and Sailing Clubhouse, its boatyard occupying a small area of land above the path.[123] The skeleton of an abandoned paddling pool, filled with pebbles, lies mid-shore, incapable now of holding on to any of the seawater that arrives to fill it twice a day.

[121] *Originally called 'The Loaf' bathing beach - from the shape of the rocks.*
Quite when and why the 'Sugar' arrived is unknown.
Before the Second World War it was a popular bathing spot with changing cubicles and a paddling pool.

[122] *The Portishead Lifeboat Trust (founded in 1995) operates independently of the RNLI which declined to take over the marine rescue service the Yacht and Sailing Club had provided up to 1992. The lifeboat trust raises funds and trains its own lifeboat personnel. Its services are frequently called upon. There are hopes it will move to a place close to the entrance of the Portishead Marina from where it will be able to launch at all states of the tide.*

[123] *I once set sail from here in a 17ft Wayfarer dinghy.*
I was the clueless crew to Captain Tony Hinchliffe who 'sailed a bit'.
His wife Mary no longer accompanied him. Why was that?
The wind was a trifle brisk and other boats were heading for shore as we headed out to sea.
"Go home!" they shouted. Well, it didn't seem that easy to turn round.
Before I knew it, we were half way to Clevedon, with me ducking and weaving to avoid the boom, and 'lee-ho-ing' while not having any idea what was going on - save that by doing it, I avoided being knocked senseless - which, come to think of it, might have been better for Tony's control of the boat. We made our way back, very slowly, along the quieter water close to the shore.
Chastened, we hauled the Wayfarer up the causeway and slipped it back into its boatyard home.
I never sailed from The Loaf beach again, and I'm not sure Tony did either.
(I found out later why Mary no longer went sailing - last time out they just about sank.
But she didn't like to say.)

Rounding a minor promontory, we arrive in Kilkenny Bay (we've done this both along the shore and by the coast path). The post-war housing estates' advance has been halted here by the golf course[124] which fills a wide acreage between Nore Road and the bay. Much of the old course has reverted to coastal meadow and there's a healthy mix of trees along the cliff line - oaks, sycamore, whitebeam, ash and wild cherry, a broad stand of Monterey pines. In late May, bright yellow bands of charlock border the pathway. Alongside the steps leading down into the bay a small stream runs, before losing itself amongst the pebbles on the shore.

[124] The golf course was designed in 1907 by Harry Vardon who had won the British Open 6 times.
Originally it covered 83 acres, beyond the Nore Road to the crest of the hill.
Much of its land has been given up to houses but a challenging 9 hole approach course remains.

Stoney Steep

In the midst of the grassland stands the remains of a windmill. It has long lost its sails and now serves as a pub[125] (The Windmill Inn) with a fantastic aspect - the broad reach of the Bristol Channel, the Welsh coast and hills. We sit on the terrace and watch the big boats go by.

A short diversion south-east of Nore Road (ie up the hill to the West Hill district) takes us to an area which, like so much of Portishead, is changing fast. Quite a few of the buildings mentioned in the 1988 Gordano Trail have gone, so it's a relief to find that the 'Stoney Steep' cottages are still there. This narrow, cobbled lane consists of two arms that fall precipitously away from the main road (close to the Moose Hall chapel) to meet at Welly Bottom where a hand pump stands and a small stream flows. It's the only access to dwellings built onto a series of quarried platforms down the hill. The tiny gardens are full of foxgloves and roses - the path weaves its way past gates and railings, the air scented with the orange-blossom of creamy flowered Philadelphus. Ivy, Red valerian and ferns spurt from the tops of crumbling stone walls. Some of the cottages appear worryingly neglected - romantic ruins. At the bottom of Stoney Steep, just beyond the hand pump and the stream and through the encircling trees, we can make out the houses on Avon Way. We turn back up the Steep, anxious to hold on to, for as long as we can, the unique atmosphere of this secret place.

[125]*Much longer a pub than a windmill. In 1907 it became the new golf course's clubhouse. John Nisbet (or Nesbitt) was allowed to build the mill in 1832, having had to relinquish his tidal mill (now the White Lion Inn in the High Street) after the enclosure of the Gordano district. The windmill turned out to be badly positioned and Nisbet left in 1846. By 1848 the wind-sails and machinery were removed and the tower became a cottage.*

The enclosing cliffs of Kilkenny Bay rise some ten metres above the beach, topped by hanging thickets of trees. The cliffs are made up of contrasting strata of red and grey stone and the red especially is dotted with sparkly pebbles of white quartz.[126] Along the shoreline, Spartina grass is forming worrying clumps, and it extends to occupy, almost entirely, Woodhill Bay a little

further north. Just beyond Kilkenny's north-east cliffs the sea-wall begins, defending a terrace of 18th century fishermen's cottages and Victorian villas - these are on a short spur from Beach Road West. Just up the road, away from the beach, we come upon charming Myrtle Cottage with its contained Regency style - a rampant white perfumed Mme. Alfred Carriere rose covers its south wall.

Myrtle Cottage

[126]*The Kilkenny rocks are Devonian Old Red sandstones - they're not always red! The quartz pebbles represent the remains of quartz strata that ran through pre-Devonian hills. The hills eroded away and the hard quartz became incorporated in the formation of new rock. (Peter Hardy)*

We have arrived at Woodhill Bay: Portishead 'the seaside resort' - although here the sea appears to have been almost abandoned, lost beyond what has become a salting of Spartina grass. The Esplanade makes a pleasing half-mile curve to the low promontory of Battery Point and its navigation light. In summer sunshine this is a delightful place with a wide area of lawns, water and trees, sheltering beneath the gentle rise of Woodhill.[127] A boating lake, tennis courts, bowling greens, a cricket ground with a pavilion and practice nets complete the scene - the only intrusion is the anomalous scar of the 1960's swimming pool, grafted onto the landward end of Battery Point.

The sea-wall runs 5 ft above the shoreline with its strawy Spartina detritus but, thankfully, the grass does eventually give out a few yards from the Point. The pebbles here are full of crinoid and seashell fossils and we find lots![128]

Pebbles from Woodhill Bay

[127] *This was originally a boggy place called the Rodmoor, certainly not a pleasure-ground. In 1910, unemployed men were brought in from Bristol to clear the scrub and drain the rhynes.*

[128] *Approaching Battery Point along the beach, there are tightly folded strata of Carboniferous Limestone (distorted during the Armorican orogeny, the time of violent earth movement, 295 million years ago, that created the Mendip Hills). Exposed along the southern face of the Point are close bands of pink and rust coloured Triassic rock.*

An easy clamber gets us to the top of the Point where, for the first time, we can see round the corner - to the mouth of the River Avon and the industrialised seaboard of Avonmouth. In May 1997, Rosie and I watched the replica sailing ship 'The Matthew' from here, as the craft set off to commemorate John Cabot's journey to Newfoundland 500 years before.[129] The deep water channel runs close to Battery Point; ships pass by at a breathtaking proximity and emphasise this small promontory's centuries-old strategic importance.[130] There's been a lighthouse here since 1931, which, until recent years, was accompanied by a fog-bell. (The light emits 3 quick flashes every 10 seconds and can be seen for 16 miles.)

Beached Bike

[129]*In 1997, Rosie created three tile paintings depicting 'The Journey and Arrival of The Matthew' for the Cabot 500 Festival. They were later purchased by the City of Bristol Museum and Art Gallery.*

[130]*There's an Iron Age camp up on Woodhill, and Battery Point which (formerly Portishead Point) may well have been a Roman Guard Station. During Elizabeth I's time, a watchtower probably stood here on the lookout for Spanish invasion. By the time of the Civil War, a fort had been built on Portishead Point housing a Royalist garrison thus "commanding the sea-way to Bristol". After two years the war moved the Parliamentary way and the garrison, threatened with 200 clubmen (good grief!), elected for a quiet retreat "much perplexed" - the men melting back into the shire. Bristol fell to the Parliamentary army a few weeks later. In 1864 the Point was refortified as a gun battery and again during World War II, with two 4.7 antisubmarine guns . (Eve Wigan and A.B.L. Reid)*

Descending from the promontory, we meander around Lake Road. Between the encircling lime trees, we can see over the cricket ground and in a corner of the field boys are practising in the nets. Higher up, along the Woodhill ridge, runs a stepped terrace of red stone houses: Adelaide Terrace, built in the 1850s.[131] The houses rise a three storeys into the gable, while to their rear (the aspect with the view, in Battery Lane) a lower-ground storey is necessary to take up the fall of the hill. These houses, as in similar hillside developments in Clevedon and Weston-super-Mare, take full advantage of the heart-stopping views across the Severn Sea with all the sunshine that's going.

[131] *Adelaide Terrace was named after Queen Adelaide (Consort of William IV) and it so happened that No.1 (now 9 Woodhill Road) was occupied by the Honourable (and Eccentric) Caroline Boyle who had been lady-in-waiting to Her Majesty for 19 years. She would surprise unwanted visitors by declaring from her window; "The Honourable Caroline Boyle is not at home!" She also surprised the local rector by taking exception to one of his sermons and marching out of the church, with maids in attendance (and in order of precedence). A short while after, she elected to join the Baptists, inviting the rejected rector to 'her dipping' (ie. baptism by immersion) - an offer he courteously declined, adding that he hoped she would not catch cold. (Eve Wigan)*

Chapter Eighteen

Bird Tree Cottage,
the High Street

When Portishead (still 'Posset' to many locals) was starting out as an aspiring 'watering place' visitors grumbled that "they could only ever get to the sea by going uphill". And it's true, for the 'resort' lies on the other side of the coastal ridge and away from the medieval village that formed around the old pill harbour.

Rosie and I walk up from the Esplanade, following Beach Road West, back past Myrtle Cottage, and over the crest to Slade Road which runs parallel to and a short distance above the High Street. Slade Road, shaded by pollarded limes, ambles along the side of the hill. It's a pleasant road of late 19th century houses on the 'up' side with mostly post-war bungalows opposite, nearly all with large and furiously flowering front gardens. A sharp turn in the road brings us to above the church, from where we turn, up over Fore Hill and then down combe-like St. Mary's Road, still a narrow, wood-banked, country lane. Half way down, sunk into the bottom of the bank, is St. Mary's Well, a small, stone chamber with a puddle of water covering the gravel in its floor.[132] It's pretty anonymous - we miss it the first time we walk by - so we're relieved to find it still there! There was once a medieval chapel to 'Our Lady at Capenor' close by, presumably linked to the disappeared Manor of Capenor whose Courthouse was demolished in 1967. A little further on down the lane we pass cream-washed Capenor Cottage, reckoned to be all that remains of the old manor.[133]

We follow St. Mary's Road on down towards the south end of the High Street. Set above the road, on its south side, is the tiny Friends' Meeting House fashioned from a cottage and neatly thatched, it has a refined austerity about it. This area was the centre of much Quaker activity during the late 17th century.[134]

[132] St. Mary's Well, also known as the Simmery Well, was once "a limpid spring of excellent water", but no more - nearby development seems to have disturbed the supply. According to Phil Quinn, the well was deemed to have 'miraculous healing powers' especially for failing eyesight - so much so that in the 1940s the water was analysed but, disappointingly, showed nothing more than a slightly raised magnesium content. The Simmery Well is also a 'pin well' (one of only 4 in the region); women anxious to bear children would attend to offer up pins to the spring - a tradition maintained up to the 1960s.

[133] Eve Wigan wondered if 'Capenor' came from 'cap noir' - Cape Black - the Black Nore Point of our day.

[134] Around 1669, Thomas Hodds donated his cottage to his fellow Quakers (among them Edmund Beakes of Greenfield Farm and Thomas Parsons of the Grange close by) - an active Society in Portishead at that time, making endless difficulties for the local religious and magisterial authorities. The Friends were threatened with 'fines, flogging and transportation' and were often turned out of their Meeting House onto the street. Thomas Parsons was consigned to Ilchester Gaol where he died of 'gaol fever' (typhus) in 1670. (Eve Wigan)

Where St. Mary's Road reaches the High Street, it is shaded by high lime trees and this part of the town, regardless of the present fever of construction, has managed to hold onto a lot of its older buildings: Bird Tree Cottage, Grange Farm, 'The Farm', as well as Clarence House - the former home of Eve Wigan (the wonderful, local historian, much quoted by me!). Mind you, Eve might be a little surprised to find her house now serving 'Spicy Aroma Tandoori'. About 500m north, we reach Church Road South - again sheltered by splendid trees, with the russet towers of the Court House and St. Peter's Church vying for the skyline.[135] We are lucky to be here in warm, early June; the gardens around the Court House are bordered by an effulgence of cream-yellow roses whose scent fills the entire road. St. Peter's beautiful Perpendicular tower rises above its well tended yard with many poignant memorials - especially sad are two gravestones listing 41 boys (aged between 12 and 15) who died while working on the training ship 'Formidable' between the years 1871 - 1901.

Despite having been prey to the 20th century, Portishead High Street remains an amiable thoroughfare, compromised at times by a heavy flow of traffic. So far, it has managed to hold onto its local businesses and there is a pleasant, busy atmosphere of people going in and out of shops. The wide pavements allow greengrocers to display plants and fruit and ironmongers their hardware. One of the town's oldest inns, 'The Poacher', still stands invitingly removed from the road[136] and there's even a Post Office, in stern, 1930s, neo-classical redbrick; it all feels just right. The High Street, north of Roath Road, becomes predominantly Victorian in character with generous pavements and an animated mix of two and three storey stone buildings, dormer and sash windows, gables and barge-boards. To the south, the tower of St. Peter's Church commands the lower slopes of Fore Hill. Looking north, the scene is dominated by the wide, green canopy of a magnificent, lone sycamore on the east pavement - sadly many splendid, mature trees have been felled in recent years (danger of falling leaves etc).

[135] St. Peter's Church, mostly 14th-15th century, was cleverly enlarged in 1878. At the same time, its original Norman font was rescued from a nearby garden by the redoubtable Miss Emma Honnywill of Church Cottage. The Court House, all that remains of the Manorial Court House, is a 16th-17th century collection of farm buildings. The hexagonal tower was added by Bristol merchant Edward Morgan as a lookout for his ships.

[136] 'The Poacher' dates from the 17th century when it looked over the village pond and the green: where the whipping post and the stocks once stood. Its latest name arose in the 1970s, before that it was known as The Anchor, The Gordon Arms and, originally, The Blew Anchor. It was the village's premier inn where all the parish meetings took place - it cost about 3 shillings (15p) in beer to get the rate signed! (Eve Wigan & A.B.L. Reid)

The north end of the High Street closes (or opens) at The White Lion Inn. Formerly a tidal mill, it gave the High Street its original name -'Old Mill Street' - and marked the south-west limit of the village's tidal creek (ie: the pill). The village was protected by a sea-wall and boats were able to sail up to the mill and the adjacent Parish Wharf with their cargoes.[137] At one time a road from the Wharf passed through an archway in the mill, part of which was incorporated into the sea-wall. Today, the White Lion is painfully constricted. Traffic lights and the wide carriageway (Wyndham Way) to the M5 press, slap-bang, up against it. It's a powerful building, with no room to breathe. And yet, on the other side of the highway, there's a surfeit of space surrounding the new structures. It represents a lost opportunity - one of Portishead's most historic buildings should have been allowed a decent setting.

[137] *A water-mill had turned close to this spot since before Domesday. It was converted to a tide mill (with a reservoir to capture the rising tide) during the 18th century, and this impeded the efficient drainage of the Gordano valley, reducing its value as pasture. Enclosure and the Weston Drainage Act 1815 resulted in the Portishead Tide Mill being put out of action. As mentioned in the previous chapter, Miller John Nesbit was compensated with a windmill on the hillside above Kilkenny Bay. The tide mill buildings were adapted for accommodation and later into an inn. Remnants of the sea-wall can be seen below the road at the inn's north-east corner and where it briefly re-emerges onto the High Street - with a millstone embedded in it.*

Crossing the wide road junction next to the White Lion, Rosie and I approach the area most changed in recent years. Not so long ago, this was an industrial landscape, home to two enormous coal-fired electrical power stations whose four towering

chimneys faced Albright & Wilson's phosphorus factory across the grey waters of the Portishead Dock. Railways, silos, workshops, coal heaps, coal ships, boats and barges. All now swept away with vast residential developments taking their place.[138]

We stand close to the remains of the old Parish Wharf, the crunch of power station ash under our feet and with the old dock stretching away before us for half a mile. It's hot, and there's little wind to fill the sails of the lone, red-sailed dinghy struggling on the water a few yards away.

We have a good view of the high-rise apartments of the Port Marine development, standing upright along the west side of the quay like so many dockside warehouses, and culminating with a lead-capped, octagonal tower - a great 'Pharos' surveilling the harbour gates and the pier approaches: the waters of the King Road.[139] Most of the harbour is now a successful marina - yachts and motorboats crowd against the pontoons while craft arrive and depart with the tides. Close to the south-west boundary of the dock is the Parish Wharf Pool fronted with pine trees. Rosie carried out a tile commission here in 1996 with paintings of underwater creatures like crabs, shells and fishes, as well as a pirate riddle to solve.

[138] *Judging from old photographs, the power station chimneys could be seen while standing on the Esplanade in Woodhill Bay - jutting above the treeline on the other side of Woodhill. Power Station A was built in 1929 with Station B following in the mid-1950s - for a while Portishead supplied half of Wessex's electrical power. They switched from coal to oil in 1972, but were phased out in 1976 (Station A) and 1982 (Station B). The last two of the four great chimney stacks (the tallest was 383 ft / 115m high) were felled with dynamite in 1992.*

[139] *The nautical meaning of 'road' is different: it's an area of sheltered water where boats may anchor in safety (OED). The King Road was often the place of departure for ships out of Bristol, where, "looking to the open sea and free of the towing men, they could shake out their sails and pray for a favourable wind." (Grahame Farr). It was on the King Road that the wooden training ship 'Formidable' was moored for 40 years.*

The Pool backs onto Station Road which once linked the High Street with the power
stations and is now a pleasant, leafy avenue. We walk in the shade of a line of magnificent
linden trees to the stations' iron gates (beautifully restored, but they no longer span the
road) which now demarcate the start of the Portishead Quays. The huge 545 acre
development now fills the western slopes of Woodhill (originally hillside meadows called
'the Saltye') from just below the trees of East Wood down to the very edge of the old
dockside quay. Despite its enormity and the din of construction, it appears to be succeeding
in creating an attractive place to live: a mix of terraced houses and cottages, high apartments
and lofty penthouses, with a lovely primary school overlooking the marina pool.

Taking South Road and an easy climb, we emerge onto a wide, open landscape where
houses and verandahs look out over a hillside park sculpted to form a grassy amphitheatre.
Five rust-red female figures perform on high cylindrical pedestals before a gallery audience
of houses that curve with the descent of the hill.[140] It's a compelling theatrical space to
which the tall apartments along the dockside form a dramatic backdrop.

[140] *The iron sculptures are by Rick Kirby, born in 1952 in Gillingham and now based in London.*

Higher up, on Woodhill, Pier Road runs along the southern margin of East Wood and the mood is quieter here with grassed verges, dove-grey houses facing the trees. The road rises and then falls to The Royal Hotel looking out over the waters of the King Road. It's a handsome, twin-gabled building (neo-Tudor) of soft-buff stone, spick and span, it belies its years.[141] Below, the pier causeway stretches into the Channel and the coastal wharfs[142] of Portbury and St. George curve to the mouth of the River Avon.

[141] *Being a short river journey from Clifton Hotwells, visitors to the Spa had the opportunity of 'water excursions' to Portishead since the 1720s. Initially boats would berth at the mouth of the Portishead Pill with the excursionists picnicking in the meadows below Woodhill. The opening of The Royal Hotel in 1831 by the Bristol Corporation (which owned much local land) proved to be a false start in the development of Portishead as a seaside resort. Despite the construction of some roads and a small landing place, after a brief flurry of building activity the Corporation ran out of steam (or interest) and Portishead did not go on to expand in the way of Clevedon or Weston-super-Mare. It was the development of the dock in 1870s that moved the small town towards a more industrial future that would last over a hundred years.*

[142] *Different spelling to the Wick and Kingston Warths, but the same sea-defence function, it appears.*

We elect to take the Woodland Road along East Wood's northern boundary. Overlooking the sea, many of Portishead's grandest and earliest houses (1830s and 40s) are found along this stretch of cliff road. One, 'The Saltings', at its western end, began life as 'The Baths' offering shower and plunge baths for 1s. 6d. and a Reading Room, complete with national newspapers.[143] Keeping up with the news and keeping clean wasn't cheap! Walking back towards The Royal, we find this road largely unspoiled, with many of the huge sycamores, planted a good while ago, being allowed to survive. Space between the houses and trees give us an easy sight of the sea and glimpses of ships pushing north-east towards the Bristol ports.

Below The Royal, steps lead us down towards the pier, past the former Dockmaster's House and what was once the railway Pier Station terminal building - a redbrick longhouse, deserted at present, but otherwise fully occupied by house martins nesting under its eaves.[144] They zoom and chitter above us, making stall-turns when they miss their nest-holes and wheeling around for a second run. Over us towers the Port Marine pharos (the signature building of post-industrial Portishead?), while before us, the jagged causeway of the pier already seems a relic of a departed era. But despite all the changes being wrought, when we look back from the pier causeway our view of the Royal Hotel - perched on the modest rise of Woodhill above a rocky cove - appears much the same as in prints of the mid-1830s.

[143]*Bond and Farndon's 1855 Portishead Guide waxes lyrical:"The attractions of this classical little structure are peculiarly enhanced by the unremitting attention bestowed on all its visitants, by its present able occupants, Mr. and Mrs. Richards. Great ingenuity has been exercised in rendering this building worthy of its name, amply evidenced by the many conveniences which are here introduced into so narrow a space; for, not only are there hot, cold, and plunging baths, dressing rooms and saloons, but also a singular contrivance, by which the discoloured waters of the Channel are converted, by filtration, into a limpid element (without losing a grain of their saline impregnation,) by a system not elsewhere introduced, but which so improves the appearance of the waters, that the clearest spring dares not boast of a brighter quality." Wow!*

[144]*Local historian Ken Crowhurst told me this was the end of the line for the original Portishead & Pier Railway Company' which opened in 1867 - the buffers were within a few yards of the sea-wall. It later became part of the Great Western Railway. The handsome GWR station was lost with the construction of the second power station in the 1950s.*

From Portishead Pier

Across from the pier, on the other side of the pill close to the entrance to the lock, is a small muddy inlet known as 'Portishead Pool' or 'The Hole'. A few boats are moored there, but in the past this was where the Bristol and Gloucester Pilots had their station and from which they would be transferred, by cutter, to ships out on the King Road or Walton Bay. With the low tide, on either side of the pier black ribs of shattered hulls finger out of the ooze. To the north-west, out across a gunmetal sea is the dark imprint of Denny Island: a suspicious nodule of land, about 4 km offshore, on the edge of the Bedwin Sands.[145]

Eastwood from the pier

[145] *Denny Island. The OED states that 'denny' means: having or abounding in dens, cavities or hollows. Other than that, the name's origin seems lost in obscurity. I haven't met anyone who's been on the island, although Grahame Farr tells the story of someone who camped there for a night and found it abounding in rats!*

The Pill at Portishead

Goldenmean leaves Portishead Lock

In 1954, when Grahame Farr (author of 'Somerset Harbours') called in on Portishead,
he was able to walk from the end of the High Street "with pleasantly shady trees",
through an archway in the White Lion Inn (the old tidal mill) and on to the Parish Wharf at the
town's harbour. Here, he looked over a scene of fevered activity: the second electricity power
station as well as a phosphorus factory were being built. Trains clanged and whistled.
Tipping trucks shunted by, filled with ash from the generating station, to the saltmarsh,
dumping grounds. He describes the Parish Wharf as having "a real West-country flavour":
coloured yachts and boats of all sizes; the remains of an old steam pilot cutter,
the 'Queen Mother'; the slap of wavelets against boats' hulls.

Continued

After the war, in 1945, there was official resistance to the harbour being reopened to small craft, even though their access was guaranteed by two Acts of Parliament going back to 1814. Indeed, that original Act of Enclosure in 1814 secured the public wharf at the half-mile long tidal pill, "with two rood of common land". The first landing place had been close to the tidal mill with the pill open to all as a 'harbour of refuge'. Coasting sloops were busy with local trade and Channel pilots also used the wharf, watchful for ships out on the sheltered anchorage of the King Road. In 1855, the Portishead Guide described "Creek vessels frequently arriving laden with coal for the supply of the Coal Wharves and cargoes of iron ore raised at Clapton for export to Wales".

Bristolians had been making river trips to Portishead for well over a century before The Royal Hotel arrived in 1830 and whose stone slipway pier began to fall apart almost as soon as it was built. After that, various proposals for new piers were put forward including, in 1839, one by Isambard Kingdom Brunel to provide a terminal for his steamship 'Great Western'. The Royal Hotel would have accommodated embarking transatlantic passengers! In the end, the railway didn't get to Portishead until 1867, with a substantial new pier following a year later. At last, passengers on steamers from Ireland and Ilfracombe (but not America) could disembark at Portishead and complete their journey to Bristol by rail, saving up to 12 hours.

In 1879 the Portishead Dock scheme was completed by widening the old pill and forming a floating harbour behind a single lock - this gave Portishead the capacity to handle much bigger ships. Unfortunately, Avonmouth had opened two years earlier and the plans for Portishead never really got going. Things looked up considerably with the construction of the first electricity power station in 1929, and the dock became an important and busy place during the Second World War. Soon after came the second power station joined by a phosphorus factory consuming enormous amounts of coal and ore - all brought in by sea.

But now, 50 years after Grahame Farr was surveying the harbour, the immense power stations and factories are gone, along with the ore bearing ships and the coal barges. It's as though they had never been. Yachts and motor cruisers, houses and apartments, now take their place, crowding in along the pill.

Chapter Nineteen

SHEEPWAY AND PORTBURY

Portishead from St. George's Wharf

East of the Portishead pier, the land lies low and flat to the mouth of the Avon River. The remains of the original sea-wall, the 'Old Sea Bank', can still be made out about half a kilometre inland, while the later construction makes a concave arc facing a wide expanse of saltmarsh and the sea. Between the two walls lie wharf pasture and wetland which is presently undergoing enormous change: building land is being raised and defended by freshly excavated gulleys and embankments, while other zones are set aside as open water and nature reserves. Two areas of moderately higher land - what Eve Wigan described as 'islands of Old Red Sandstone' - interrupt this alluvial plain on either side of the small creek known as St. George's Pill.

Royal Portbury pier from St. George's Wharf

The eastern rise, once surmounted by Sheephouse Farm, has now been absorbed
into the Royal Portbury Dock, while to the west, the linear hamlet of Sheepway
bestrides the other rise. These areas nearly always remained free of flood and were
safe for the raising of sheep.[146]

The road to Sheepway peels off the A369, the main road linking Portishead with
the M5 motorway. Houses and cottages lie scattered along both sides of the Sheepway
road, with one or two footpaths pressing on down to the coast. The hedgerows are
high, obscuring the level acres of grassland and large open fields. We leave the car
close to Atherton House and walk on down the grassy track that leads to the shore.
Breaks in the hedges reveal the wooded slopes of the Clevedon / Portishead ridge
and the quayside development of Port Marine. Above us, electricity pylons stride out
across the levels, but the shoreline remains hidden until we climb over the outer sea-
wall. Wide saltings stretch away, halted in the east by the pier guarding the entrance
to the Royal Portbury Dock and its cranes and gantries. Huge container ships tower
above the dockside.

Much of the area where we're standing is now a 'wildlife corridor' securing a
green-belt link between the Gordano valley and the coast. And it needs to be,
for the development pressure on this area is huge (at the moment, it is one of Britain's
most rapidly expanding places for housing and industry) and these alluvial flood-plains
have to be protected: for the animals and plants that inhabit them, and as a defence
against future inundation.

[146] *Sheepway (or Sheepey) probably means the 'island of sheep'.*
Some old maps give it as 'Shipway' with a Roman causeway linking it to Portbury and Conygar Hill.
Just to confuse things 'Sheephouse' may have arisen from 'Shiphorse',
the stable for the heavy horses used for hauling ships up and down the Avon.
(Eve Wigan & A.B.L. Reid)

In a previous life, the Sheepway road was itself the A369, the main road from Portishead to Bristol through Portbury and Easton-in-Gordano. The road crosses a stone railway bridge above the old Portbury station and the route of the line is still there, although plans to reopen the rail link are, at present, stalled. If you're on foot or bicycle, there is still direct access to Portbury by a footbridge that crosses both the main road and the motorway in one giant leap. And it's a noisy crossing although, to our surprise, the motorway roar is dramatically subdued once we are in the village. From the footbridge we can look straight up the High Street to the conical mound of Conygar Hill (now girded by detached houses) with the square rust-stone tower of the Old Priory squatting at its foot.[147] We absentmindedly wander westwards, past the priory and up a footpath through Prior's Wood where we come upon the romantic ruin of an exquisite, small, Gothic cottage. What has led to its abandonment? Presumably the machinations of a large estate which no longer had the need to house a gamekeeper or woodsman.

The Gothic cottage,
Portbury

[147]*Until 1972, the Old Priory served as the village school for a hundred years. It's a fragment of the medieval priory which once occupied the heart of the village - a cell of the Augustinian Bromore Priory in Hampshire. The priory was broken up with the Dissolution of the Monasteries in 1536. The present building is thought to be early Tudor, much restored in the 19th century. The school is now west of the village, close to St. Mary's Church.*

Venerable Portbury has lost much of its shape and character with the imposition of the motorway and post-war development. The road scythes through the village's northern and western boundaries disconnecting it from the rest of Gordano, as well as pulling in an unfair burden of traffic. St. Mary's Church stands a short way off from the village and surrounded by fields. Ignoring the fractious row of the M5, we take a wonderful approach to the church across an open meadow (part of what was once called the Great Common Mead) with the outliers to wooded Windmill Hill rising behind. The church stands surrounded by ancient yews and its gravestones share the same lecturing tone (they don't half go on!) as those in Clapton and elsewhere round 'ere. Between St. Mary's and the village school is a small open area with a grassed hummock on which has been positioned the Portbury Standing Stone. It's a splendid, lichen-encrusted lozenge that had stood (for some 4,000 years!) in a field behind the church. In the 1950s it was dug up and used to fill a pond, remaining there until it was rescued and placed, fittingly, between its two juniors: the Norman church and the school.[148]

The Standing Stone

[148] *The Standing Stone is probably Neolithic, ie around 2000 BC, made from Dolomitic Conglomerate which may well have come from nearby Conygar Hill. St. Mary's Church is Norman, parts of which go back to the early 12th century. The 'new' village school opened in 1972. During excavations for the school, the site of a Romano-British temple, 200-500 AD, were uncovered. (Rita Summerfield).*

We walk down the lane alongside the church and past Church Cottage, returning to the main road to take the footpath which ascends between Bulling's and Longlands Woods to Windmill Hill. After crossing the fields, the path runs into a deep lane (Failand Lane) walled with elder, red campion, bracken and bramble. Amongst the tangle of undergrowth, where the footpath leaves the road again, there are the masonry remains of a gatehouse to the Berkeley manor house which once stood atop Windmill Hill.[149] We enter a curious, dark, wooded gulley called Oakham Spinney from which we break free into a field leading up to the birch woods on Windmill Hill. We are surrounded by views to the Severn Estuary and the docks, woodlands and rolling hills, copses and farms. It's July and the path folds through a hayfield of softest gold, silken grass caught in a shifting of sunshine and cloud shadow. Below, where the hay has already been cut, the cropped fields seem spiritless and still, while all about us the grass, brushed by the wind, is alive.

[149]*A fortified manor house, it was built around 1145 and was occupied by a sequence of Lord Berkeleys from 'Robert the Devout' to 'Henry the Harmless' - who died in 1613 from 'a surfeit of small custards'. These were the Berkeleys of Berkeley Castle in Gloucestershire, and the Portbury Hundred was an important part of their estate. The Berkeleys seem to have divided their time between feasting and jousting in Somerset and Gloucestershire, and fighting a variety of wars against the Welsh, Scots and French. (Eve Wigan & A.B.L.Reid)*

Chapter Twenty

Both sides of the mouth of the River Avon are off limits to the shoreline stroller. The gigantic docking facilities of Royal Portbury in Somerset, and at Avonmouth on the Gloucestershire side have taken over large areas of river-mouth land and access to it is carefully controlled.[150] We had tried riding our bikes to take a look from the motorway bridge, but the cycle track is on the landward side which meant the docks remained hidden from view. So the only option is to go by sea! During the summer months the *M. V. Balmoral* makes several journeys from Clevedon Pier, up the River Avon to the Bristol Docks. So we took a trip, which we'll pick up at Portishead.

North and South Pier lighthouses, Avonmouth

[150] *We were shown round Royal Portbury by Patrick Kearon of the Bristol Port Company, which took over the docks from the Bristol City Council in 1991. It's an enormous area of enclosed water capable of handling the gigantic present day container ships and bulk carriers. While we were there, the bulk carrier Regina was the biggest ship in dock, moored at Berth 6 disgorging coal. Despite the working industrial landscape, the company is setting aside land and creating green corridors for wild life. Recently they succeeded in attracting three pairs of barn owls to nesting boxes placed around the port.*

From the Swash Channel

Rounding Portishead's Battery Point, *Balmoral* follows the deep waterchannel which passes close to the northern side of the promontory. We are now in the famed King Road (described in the previous chapter) where once so many ships anchored in preparation to enter or take their leave of Bristol. The arm of Portishead Pier stretches out to us, with the bright, pastel towers of the Port Marine development rising behind. A featureless saltmarsh, bounding the Portbury and St. George's Wharves, reaches all the way to the Avon's mouth - which we are approaching several hours before high water. *Balmoral* keeps the green conical Firefly buoy (named after the rocks it guards against) to starboard and swings out further into the King Road.

The Firefly buoy

Within a short time we can make out the river's mouth (not easy in this horizontal landscape), demarcated by the long causeway of Royal Portbury's East Pier and Avonmouth's South Pier lighthouse.[151] There was once an island here, Dumball Island, just north-west of the river-mouth, before the docks consumed it over a century ago.[152] These days it's the South Pier that forms the river's northern entrance and we enter close to that side, sailing in the deeper water of the Swash Channel.

From the upper deck of the *Balmoral,* we can just make out the docklands accompanied, on the Somerset side, by silos and serried ranks of newly imported cars. The Avonmouth bridge rises in a great arch above us, an unadorned structure of functional modernity, its massive pairs of concrete pillars, planted deep into the estuarine ooze, march into the distance like shapes seen in opposing mirrors. Saltmarsh accompanies the river on both sides with a few muddy creeks and muddy boats along the way. We are moving quite quickly now as the rising tide and *Balmoral's* engines carry us briskly up river.

Royal Portbury owl nesting box

[151]*Avonmouth docks have two lighthouses: one on each of its two piers, north and south. These are known as the Norwegian-stone lighthouses (they're built from Norwegian granite) and in 1908 they replaced the Avon Lighthouse which had shone since 1840, long before the docks came into being. The lighthouses are not identical: the north light is taller (50ft and visible for 18 miles) than its rather squat sibling on the south pier-head (30ft high and visible for 10 miles).*

[152] *'Dung Ball Island' on old maps. The island disappeared at the beginning of the 20th century when the Prince Edward Dock was constructed. It was notoriously vulnerable to flood and there were times when it virtually sank beneath the waves. Its other claim to notoriety was the Gibbet Pole. In 1761 the Bristol Corporation paid £22.19s.6d for the construction of a gibbet on the island's shore to dangle the iron-caged corpse of murderer Pat Ward before approaching ships "to strike terror into lawless sailors". The gibbet pole remained there (but not Pat Ward) for a further 120 years. (Ethel Thomas)*

*The harbour
at Pill*

The saltings extend 200 metres or so back from the river bank and the first houses of
Pill lie immediately beyond that, defended by a grassed embankment that follows the line
of the Old Sea Bank.[153] There's a photograph in one of John Rich's books about Pill,
showing the village at the turn of the 19th and 20th centuries, and taken from the
Shirehampton side. The river is at mid-tide and the ferryboat waits at the bottom of the
Pill slipway on which a small child stands. The houses and pubs press up to the side of the
river and crowd the side of the hill - a wonderful jumble of eaves, gables and dormer
windows. Sadly, much of that hospitable clutter was swept away after the Second World
War when many cottages were deemed unfit for habitation.[154] They were replaced by
well-intended but unsympathetic 1960s municipal housing devoid of any local personality.

[153]*Started out as 'Crockerne Pill' but by the early 17th century had become simply 'Pill'. The huge importance of the
inlet as a maritime base and for ship building etc. had made its name locally self-evident.
(Pill is a term for a small tidal creek used on both sides of the Bristol Channel). OED.*

[154]*Life could be pretty grim. Flooding was a perennial problem, liable to happen four to five times a year at the time of
the equinox - in March and September when the spring tides are at their highest. Heavy rain and westerly winds could
make things much worse. Flood water could reach well beyond the railway viaduct. Sand-bags and flood-boards across
doorways helped; it was just when water came through the downstairs windows that things got a little more awkward.
The ground floors of pubs and houses would fill with water, so the trick was to move furniture swiftly upstairs.
Flagstone floors made cleaning up the slime a little easier.*

From its very beginnings the port of Bristol needed men to guide, tow and haul shipping from the mouth of the tortuous River Avon to the docks at its heart. The creek of Crockerne Pill was perfectly placed and a fiercely independent community of mariners evolved there. For centuries the merchants and the Bristol Corporation tried to bring the men of Pill under their aegis but it was strongly resisted, although the licensing of Bristol Channel pilots appears to have begun in the early 18th century.

It might be best now to allow *M. V. Balmoral* to proceed gracefully upstream while Rosie and I continue these final few miles of the Somerset seaboard on foot (and bike). We can always hop back on board from time to time when it suits!

Happily, Pill is not the place the view from the *Balmoral* suggests: many of the cottages and houses on the hillside survive and bear testimony to how self-contained the village once was. Walking around with John Rich (historian and former Bristol pilot), it seems as though half the cottages have had previous lives as public houses.[155] "There's the brewery and there's the abattoir" John tells us. "There's the Stuckey's Bank. And that was a bakery - the baker used to seal the oven with sausages of dough that baked to a delicious crunch. Children who did errands for him had them as a reward." We walk past twin-bayed Victorian villas and houses steeply stacked on the side of the hill, eventually crossing the deep cut of the railway line and down Back Lane to Pump Square, on the very edge of the river and the creek.

The mansard-roofed headquarters of the Portishead Cruising Club stand on the west side of Pill's creek-mouth, punts and dinghys stacked on their sterns along the cobbled jetty.[156] The old ferry slipway slopes to the river close by and its sister slips out of the river on the Shirehampton side. For centuries, this was the only ferry crossing across the Avon until you got to Bristol.[157]

[155]*In spite of its reputation the village had, at most, 18 pubs at any one time - which didn't compare with Bristol's 50 on its quay alone!*

[156]*Their base in Portishead Dock was closed to them during the Second World War, so they moved to Pill. And they've never gone back. Their headquarters stand on the site of the old Waterloo Inn where, on a flood tide, the water could reach up to the piano keyboard or even half way up the dartboard (good story). Mind you, the dartboard was so placed it was a legal shot to go in off the ceiling for a double-top! (John Rich)*

All that changed with the arrival of the Avonmouth bridge in 1972 which provided a cycle-way and footpath to the Gloucestershire side. The folk who had once used the ferry drifted away and it closed in 1974. Facing the Sailing Club across the pill is the stern Custom's Watch House, erected in the 18th century to deal with suspected smuggling.[158] Next to the Watch House was where 'Rowles' Boatyard' once built many Bristol pilots' skiffs and cutters. John Rich points out to us two surviving hobblers' boats moored at the mouth of the creek - sharp bowed with rowlocks for four pairs of oars. (See Special Page)

The flood defences of 1993 have improved security against flood-tides enormously - although they did fail in 1997 when someone forgot to close the flood gate! The sea-wall, with substantial semicircular capping-stones, runs the length of Marine Parade and closes at a huge sea anchor (donated by the Bristol Port Authority) embedded in the pavement. We walk along the west side of the creek, passing the Duke of Cornwall (one of the few buildings in John Rich's photograph still standing) on the other side of Pump Square. As well as the hobblers' boats, the inlet is filled with yachts in fine fettle - although one, with its sailing days pretty much over, lies on its starboard side, its mast at a 40 degree angle across the pill.

The creek ends at a sluice gate which controls the waters of the culverted Crockerne stream. Above it rises a grassy slope of made ground upon which rests a comfortable seat and a celebratory plaque or two.[159] Immediately beyond, a great red-brick railway viaduct carves its way across the inlet's shallow combe - like it's landed from an alien industrial landscape, appearing from nowhere and then disappearing into the hillside behind The Star Inn. An old bench loiters in the sunshine under one of the arches. Squeezed in on the viaduct's south side, there is Victoria Park, a curiously quiet place crowded with lime trees and planes. A group of red tiled cottages, raised above the road, hint at what used to be here.

[157]Historian Eve Wigan deliciously describes:"the way my lord of Berkeley would come riding from Gloucestershire, crossing the Avon at Crooken Pill and winding through Easton along Lodway, up Combe Lane and past Honor Farm." and thence to Portbury.

[158]The merchants and Corporation of Bristol developed a degree of paranoid hostility to the Pill mariners who refused to kowtow to 'authority'. Pill was a proud, tough, closed community and whatever illicit importing went on, well... it was only their due.

[159]The plaques mark Pilot James Ray setting sail to assist the 'Matthew' in 1497 (see Special Page) and the departure for America of Methodist ministers Francis Asbury in 1771 and Thomas Coke in 1784.

What Charlotte Clarke had to say...

In 1755, Charlotte Clarke wrote: "With the necessary utensils from the
Pastry Cook's shop and the friendly assistance of our good friends we took leave
and set out for a little place called Pill, a sort of harbour for ships five miles this side of Bristol."
But it clearly didn't suit! "The place itself is not unpleasant if it were
inhabited by any other kind of people than the savages whom infest it and
are only in outward form distinguished from 'Beasts of Prey'.

"To be short, the villainies of these wretches are of so heinous and uncivilised
a nature they render the place so unlike any other part of the habitable
world that I can only compare it to the Ante chamber of that abode we are admonished
to avoid in the next life by leading a good one here.

"A boy of eight or ten years is so well versed in the most beastly discourse
and the most dreadful sin of blasphemy and swearing as any drunken reprobate
of 30 and he who drinks hardest and excels most in these terrible qualifications
stands best in his father's favour.

"There are some few that don't belong to the boats that are reasonable
creatures and I am amazed that they can patiently bear to reside where there
are such a numerous set of cannibals, - a name they justly deserve,
for I believe there are some among them who would not scruple
to make a meal of their fellow creatures."

(Thanks to John Rich for this!)

At the Sailing Club jetty, leaning on the sea-wall, we look up-river where the stream follows a gentle, north-easterly curve for about a mile or so. This stretch of the Avon (and the Somerset side especially) was, for many hundreds of years, vital to the successful operation of the Port of Bristol and earned itself the title of 'The Hung Road'.[160] Many ships would anchor here and go no further. It's invisible from the land so we return to the river...

Back on the *Balmoral,* we are able to see the low cliff face of a sunless river bank draped in dark seaweed. In the trees along the cliff-top are perched ghosty herons, like the wraiths of lost mariners waiting for ships that will never return. About half way along the Hung Road, the boat passes a semicircular whitewashed landing-place, fronted by two brick columns and a small archway at the centre of the curved wall. It probably served as a water-gate to the Ham Green estate.[161] These days the left tower is topped by a white navigation light. The curve of the Hung Road ends at the small creek of Chapel Pill and, as *Balmoral* enters the infamous Horseshoe Bend, the low cliffs on Somerset's side give way to open meadow.

[160] *The Hung Road was a critical area of harbourage.*
Ships either too big or reluctant to risk the hazardous Avon channel any further
could set down here and unload into or receive supplies from smaller craft.
The faster flow along the Somerset side scours the river bed, keeping the water deep and relatively free of mud.
Another factor is the rocky cliff-side to the river here. It meant ships could anchor close to the bank with their masts
tethered ('hung') to iron mooring rings set into the cliff,
preventing them from toppling at low tide.

[161] *Called 'The Folly' or 'Adam & Eve' - apparently there are two figures mounted either side of the arch,*
although Rosie and I couldn't see them from the Balmoral. During Ham Green's time as a hospital
(see later footnote), nurses would come here to sit and dabble their feet in the river at high tide -
to be joined, at times, by boys swimming across from the Shirehampton side!
Tragically, in the 1920s two nurses were swept away in the wash of a passing steamer and drowned.
(Gerald S. Hart)

Pilots, hobblers and westernmen

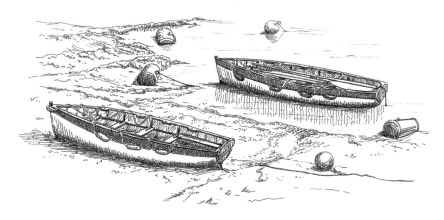

Hobblers' boats

In times past, the course of the River Avon was a mile longer from its mouth to the Bristol quays than it is today. As boats got bigger, it became increasingly problematic for them to negotiate the twisting, mud-banked, four mile journey, and local knowledge was needed more and more. Boats could only make their entrances and exits on the rising tide (to do so with the tide falling was far too hazardous) so time and daylight were of the essence. Sail power was useless and the merchant ships had to rely on being towed to and from the sea. This was carried out by the hobblers (who pulled the ships from the towpath and carried the mooring lines in their boats from ship to shore) and the tow-boatmen (up to nine small boats with eight oarsmen apiece), heaving the heavily laden merchant-ships along the river. Difficult to imagine the effort involved when heading out of Bristol with the current against you on the rising tide.

Horses were also used along the towpath on the Somerset side, with oxen coming into play if the going was soft and muddy. It could all take several days, and the journey would have to be carefully planned so that a ship wasn't stranded mid-channel with the danger of breaking its back or completely obstructing the river. (In 1579, 'the Lion' broke her moorings at the Hung Road, turned over and blocked the river for a year!) This was something the Bristol Corporation and the Merchant Venturers were ever-fearful of, and was one of the reasons the docks abandoned their city home for the ports at Avonmouth and Royal Portbury.

Continued

The Bristol Channel is one of the world's most challenging sea-ways with a huge tidal rise and fall, a powerful tide-race and unpredictable weather. The need for seafarers familiar with these fearsome waters was recognised early on, and so the guardians of the River Avon, the men of Crockerne Pill, became the natural custodians of the role of Bristol Pilot. Clearly the job evolved but there's a tradition that the 'first' pilot was James George Ray, appointed in May 1497 by the Mayor and Corporation to pilot John Cabot's *Matthew*, setting sail to discover Newfoundland. James Ray was a man of Crockerne Pill. Eventually, pilots with their assistant *'westernmen'* were to go 'seeking downalong' - as far out as Lundy Island and even Land's End to direct ships into Bristol - and, to a man, they all came from Pill.

The early boats were known as 'skiffs' or 'yawls', relatively small (around 36 ft) open craft with virtually no protection for the men on board. It's difficult to imagine anything tougher than being on such a boat in mid-winter, out beyond the Holms and Lundy, expectantly "seeking". And if no ship appeared - not exceptional given the intense competition - then no-one got paid.

During the 19th century the pilot boats developed into the classic Bristol Channel pilot cutters, with an overall length of 40 - 50ft, which are sailed and treasured to this day. These boats were fast and beautiful, a source of intense pride to the village of Pill where many of them were built - Edwin Rowles' yard continued to build boats up to 1910. In 1918 the Bristol pilots amalgamated but it wasn't until 1922 they gave up their sailing cutters for steam. Within a few years the Bristol pilotage 'district' had contracted: first to Lundy, then to the Holms and finally the King Road off Portishead. Following the amalgamation the number of pilots fell to 36, drifting down to the 15 of the present day - a few of whom still live in Pill

Much of this passage has been gleaned from the superbly researched books of John Rich (a retired Bristol Pilot of Pill) and Peter Stuckey - both listed in the Bibliography.

Chapter Twenty One

HAM GREEN TO THE HOTWELLS' LOCK

Ham Green Lake

Leaving Pill, we take the footpath that leads from behind the old Custom Watch House to the top of the grassy incline known as Watch-house Hill. From here, we can look north-west, over the village, to where the Avon snakes beneath the wide, flat parabola of the motorway bridge - a jag of pylons and a glitter of the Severn Sea beyond. The path passes beside an orchard and meets up with a cycle-track that leaves Pill close by the railway viaduct.

The cycle-track courses through Pill's new housing estate around The Green and traces the grounds of what was, up until fairly recently, Ham Green Hospital.[162] In 1959, the remains of a medieval pottery were discovered in the hospital grounds and since then 'Ham Green Ware' has turned up as far away as Dublin and the British Museum![163] As Rosie and I pass by, Ham Green House is surrounded by scaffolding and areas of the estate are in the process of being 'developed'.

From the old hospital entrance there's a gentle descent down the side of a small valley with a few cottages sprinkled along the way. In the valley floor we can see a lake tightly surrounded by trees with a wooden jetty extending to its centre, and which our path eventually passes close by. In August, the lake is speckled with yellow water lilies. Ham Green Lake was created in the landscaping of the estate in the 18th century. Water is still retained by a red stone wall, with a secondary wall and sluice controlling the outflow to the brook that flows on to Chapel Pill.

[162] *Originally 'Ham Green House', it was built in the early 1700s and later occupied by the Bright family, wealthy West India sugar merchants. Even then it had a strong medical connection: it was the birthplace and childhood home of Richard Bright, a doctor who applied scientific discipline to the art of medicine (in 1836, he described the acute and chronic forms of kidney inflammation: 'Bright's disease'). The estate was bought by the Bristol Corporation in 1893 and converted into an isolation hospital (prior to that, a hulk moored in the River Avon had provided 'accommodation for fevers'). With the NHS, it continued to specialise in the study and treatment of infectious disease (particularly tuberculosis and poliomyelitis) but broadened into other specialities after 1969. The hospital closed in 1993. (Read Gerald Hart's touching account in 'Ham Green'.)*

[163] *A pile of failed pot firings (wasters) and a kiln were discovered and dated to the 13th century. Two pot types were found: fine green-glaze ware and a greyish domestic form. Amazingly, it was discovered that a 'Knight Jug' (a characteristic late-13th century design) on display in the British Museum had come from the Ham Green pottery. It has been speculated that the 'crock' in Crockerne Pill was from the same root as 'crockery' - implying the importance of the pottery in medieval times. Ham Green ware can be seen at Bristol Museum. (Gerald Hart)*

From the horse chestnut trees at the foot of the lake, the path opens out to Chapel Pill Farm. On the two occasions we cycled this way in late summer, the blackberries were so succulent they stay in the memory - juicy and sweet with just a touch of acidity. Too good to take home, best sipped straight from the briar! The path leaves the farm with a wide field curving uphill to the south and then turns back towards the Avon alongside Chapel Pill.[164] Through breaks in the trees and undergrowth it's possible to scramble to the edge of the inlet (while avoiding a deeply dug badger set) which marks the eastern limit of the Hung Road. These days the pill provides a haven to a few yachts - but there's no tow-boatmen to haul them to the open sea.

A comfortable seat

A short distance from Chapel Pill the river starts on a violent loop known as 'Horseshoe Bend' and the cliffs of the Somerset side give way to reed beds and a few tiny creeks. This part of the cycle-way was clearly once a tow-path, for set at regular intervals along the track are substantial iron mooring-bollards that provided anchorage points for ships in difficulty, and something similar may once have aided the hobblers. These days they double up as comfortable seats, with just enough room for two. Grahame Farr describes this part of the river as having the added problem of fog - it can form quickly and without warning; in 1929 thirteen steamers got stranded! A fairly recent casualty was the paddle-steamer Waverley which grounded at the Horseshoe Bend in 1998. A little farther, on the other side of the river, is a striking whitewashed slate-roofed building with similar 18th century architecture to Pill's Custom Watch House. It has a landing platform and a small crane standing above the river. It is known as the Powder House and was where a ship's explosives had to be stored before entering Bristol.[165]

[164] *Also known as St. Katherine's Pill, referring to the chantry chapel the Berkeley family placed here in 1346. Seafarers would place votive offerings to the saint for their safe journeyings and, as with the Hung Road, ships would harbour here awaiting the tide and favourable winds. In 1547, during the Reformation, the chapel was suppressed and the lead from its roof, its two bells, chalices and ornaments sold off. Nowadays, no-one knows where it stood, although the site of Chapel Pill Farm seems likely.*

[165] *Before entering the crowded port of Bristol, ships would have to discharge their supplies of gunpowder. It was collected by much smaller boats that could come alongside the 'Gunpowder Magazine' and by allowing themselves to ground with the falling tide their dangerous cargoes could be unloaded and stored in relative safety.*

Rosie and I always enjoy cycling along this stretch of the Avon way - it feels bright and open, with an uninterrupted view over the river. We watch a lone canal-boat softly drumming past - the boatman, with one hand on the tiller while reading a book, keeps a perfect course, disappearing as the river-bend angles to the east. Across the river lies Sea Mills Reach, where the River Trym joins the Avon beneath a rusting 19th century railway viaduct and the stone arches of the Portway road.[166] At regular intervals along the river bank are white navigation lights: some on stilts above the marshy ground, others perched on the low cliffs amongst the trees. From the towpath we can see them against the dark tree canopy of Leigh Woods which cloaks the Somerset side from here to the Avon Gorge and inland to Leigh Court and Abbots Leigh.[167]

Navigation lights at Miles' Barge Dock

[166]*One of Britain's earliest 'wet docks' was sited at Sea Mills. Completed in 1715,*
it provided a floating harbour but was defeated by the lack of a good road to Bristol.
For a while it was used for the fitting out of privateers (legalised pirates) and as a whaling station. (Ethel Thomas)

[167]*Leigh Woods are now owned by the Forestry Commission (north section) and the National Trust (south section).*
In 1814 Humphrey Repton configured the woodland as part of the landscaping of the Leigh Court estate.
His woodland rides have been restored by the Forestry Commission.

The cycle-path dips beneath the trees and straightaway we are missing the sunshine we left behind on the towpath. The river bank cliffs return, and the river is glimpsed through the trees with the path in deep shadow. Trains rattle unseen over a railway viaduct below which, in Stygian dankness, lie the remains of a 19th century barge dock.[168] The path continues below the high viaduct wall through which the trunks of trees burst gasping for light. Every now and then a cutting or a combe allows some sunlight to percolate on to the track and in places the railway embankment is penetrated by tunnels to small abandoned quarries. Actually it isn't that gloomy - in summer it's more a dappled shade. Part of 'the problem' is the bright light reflecting from the high quarried rock faces on the other side of the river which deepens the sense of shadow.

We are now approaching the Avon Gorge where the cycle-way runs not far above the river.[169] We stop awhile to applaud the small vineyard, planted, by a University colleague of mine, into a cleft in the rock face on the other side of the river and defended by a high stone wall - in the early afternoon it is bathed in sunlight. From where we are standing, the rows of vines appear to scale a near vertical slope. The sides of the Gorge are coming together now and the susurrus of traffic more insistent. Suddenly, the Somerset pier of Brunel's Clifton Suspension Bridge[170] emerges above the treeline and sunlight spills onto the path where the woods have eased back from the river.

[168] *Miles' Barge Dock. Originally constructed in 1814 by Philip John Miles in order to import Bath stone for his new mansion at Leigh Court. The dock was in use 20 years later when Old Red Sandstone was quarried from the estate for the huge base pier on the Somerset side of the Clifton Suspension Bridge. In the early 20th century the dock was in use once again when strontium ore was discovered on the estate.*

[169] *I should have liked a footnote here on the formation and geology of the Avon Gorge. But it's so complicated! If you need to know, get hold of 'Nature in Avon', The Proceeding of the Bristol Naturalists' Society, Volume 47, 1987.*

[170] *The idea of a stone bridge across the Avon Gorge was first mooted by William Vick in 1700 - despite the fact that it wouldn't have gone anywhere important. He left £1000 for this purpose in his will and which had increased to £8000 by the time a series of competitions had decided on I.K. Brunel's 'Egyptian thing'. Work started in 1831 but the Bristol Riots and general economic depression caused dreadful delays. By 1843, the towers stood ready for their chains. But once again the money ran out. Brunel died in 1859. Ironically his death renewed interest for it was felt the bridge would be a splendid memorial to the great designer-engineer. Engineers W.H. Barlow (he of Clevedon Pier's 'Barlow Rails') and Sir John Hawkshaw, with the Clifton trustees, formed a new bridge company. Providentially, the chains from Brunel's London Hungerford Bridge were available and everything came together. The Clifton Suspension Bridge was opened on December 8th 1864. It had taken 33 years.*

The vast, sandstone pier of the bridge is soon above us: a massive extension of the Somerset side of the Gorge from which the suspended roadway reaches over to Clifton. Only from below can you understand the powerful underpinning of this beautiful and seemingly delicate structure. Rosie and I once lived in Clifton, in a basement flat in Royal York Crescent where the bath water, from every flat above us, gurgled its way into our bath. We walked across the bridge many times and, like everyone, wondered at the graceful economy of Brunel's design.

'Reg's Story'

Now I have a curious connection with the Clifton Suspension Bridge through the chap
who works the allotment plot next to mine in Worle: Mr 'Reg the Veg' Coombs.
Leaning on his hoe, he told me that in September 1896, at 5 o'clock in the morning,
his great-great grandfather, James Hazell (a Pill hobbler), was rowing his boat on a full
tide below the suspension bridge, when he heard two loud splashes in the water close-
by. Rowing quickly to see what was going on, he came upon two children in the river
whom he was able to lift into his boat. They were Ruby (aged 12) and Elsie Brown
(aged 3) and they had been thrown the 240 ft from the bridge by their father Charles
Brown. He was a Birmingham grocer facing bankruptcy who was later adjudged to be
insane and committed to an asylum. Amazingly, Elsie had only suffered minor leg
injuries and Ruby some spinal damage - they both made a full physical recovery.
The mental contusions, I'm sure, would have gone far deeper.

Reg's story didn't end there. It turns out that in the early 19th century,
James Hazell's father, Joseph (who lived in Pill), was press-ganged and taken on board
the man 'o war *Russell* harbouring in the King Road, off Portishead. The *Russell* then
set sail for Plymouth. Meanwhile, back home in Pill, Joseph's wife was having none of
it. She was a skilled seamstress and she set about making a sailor's uniform for herself.
She then walked to Plymouth wearing the naval kit under her own clothes and boarded
the Russell to visit her husband. Once they were alone she dressed Joseph in her
woman's clothes and pushed him ashore. She continued the disguise for ten days while
her husband walked home to Pill. As soon as she could be sure he was safe, she
revealed who she was to the surprised naval officers and was ordered from the boat.
It's astonishing what a chat down the allotments will turn up!

We are slowly running out of Somerset, pedalling through the puddles from the previous night's rain. Ineluctably, Bristol starts to impose itself with the high ranks of Clifton terraces scaling the city side of the Gorge. Up river, we can see the stern redbrick barracks of the tobacco warehouses presiding over the harbour. On the opposite bank, the wooden paddle-steamer jetties are quietly mouldering, and above the tight terraces of houses along the Hotwells Road rises the extraordinary, sandstone bulwark below Windsor Terrace. Downstream of the Hotwells Lock the divided river regroups. On our *Balmoral* journey the ship pauses here for a while, to pick up passengers from the Cumberland Basin quay, before sailing on into the harbour with all the city before her.

Across the River Avon to Clifton Hill

We cycle over the Somerset border and down onto an area of parkland below the Avon Bridge. Weeping willows grace the river bank and from the river's elbow, Rosie and I can just make out our first home together, high up on Clifton Hill.

EPILOGUE

At the hill's edge, the wood ends abruptly
But still surrounds me.
From the Old Pier, the late-night steamer plunders
The firm, still water of the Channel.

BIBLIOGRAPHY

Aston, M. & Burrow I. 1982, The Archaeology of Somerset
Beisly, Philip, 1996, The Northmarsh of Somerset
Bond & Fardon, 1855, The Portishead Guide and Visitor's Hand-book
Brown, Brian and Loosley, John, 1982, The Book of Portishead
Clevedon Civic Society, 1981, The Annals of Clevedon
Clevedon Civic Society, 1981, Clevedon from the Village to the Town
Clevedon Civic Society, 1993, Clevedon Past
Clevedon Civic Society, 1998, Clevedon's Social and Industrial Heritage
Coombes, Nigel, 1995, White Funnel Magic
Congresbury History Group, 1985, Congresbury Pubs and Inns
Congresbury History Group, 1986, The Railway at Congresbury
Congresbury History Group, 1988, Congresbury Trades
Congresbury History Group, 2002, Congresbury as 'twas
Collinson, J. 1791, The History and Antiquities of the County of Somerset
Cran, Alex S. 1983, The Story of Congresbury
Crowhurst, Ken, 2001, Portishead (Images of England)
Cumberlidge, Peter, 1988, Bristol Channel & Severn Pilot
Dymond, Charles W. 1902, Worlebury
Eglinton, Edmund, 1982, The last of the Sailing Coasters
Evans, William, 2002, Abbots Leigh - A Village History
Farr, Grahame, 1954, Somerset Harbours
Farr, Grahame, 1966, Wreck and Rescue in the Bristol Channel
Farr, M. Lovell, R. Maggs, C. & Whetmath, C. The Wrington Vale Light Railway
Gardner, Keith S. 1998, Who Made the Land Yeo?
Gordano Society, 1987-1997, Trails in Gordano Nos. 1 - 10
Greenhalgh, John & Newman, Paul, 1980, Channel Portraits
Greig Smith, James, 1898, Woodspring
Harper, Charles G. 1909, The Somerset Coast
Hart, Gerald S. 1999, Ham Green
Holt, Alan L. 1987, Old North Somerset
Jackson, L. & W. 1877, Visitor's Handbook to Weston-super-Mare
Jenkins, Linda & Redman, Sandra, 2003, The Story of Wick St. Lawrence
Knight, Francis A. 1902, The Seaboard of Mendip
Lawrence, Berta, 1970, Coleridge and Wordsworth in Somerset
Lilly, Derek and Lilly, Jane, 2000, The Builders of Clevedon
Lilly, Jane, 1990, Clevedon in Old Photographs
Lilly, Jane, 2002, The Shops on the Hill (Clevedon History Series)
Lilly, Jane, 2004, Clevedon Photographic Memories
Macleay, John, 2001, Old Portishead
Maggs, Colin G. 1990, The Weston, Clevedon & Portishead Light Railway
Mallory, Keith, 1981, Clevedon Pier
Mayberry, Tom, 2000, Coleridge and Wordsworth, The Crucible of Friendship
Mitchell, Alan, 1978, Trees of Britain and Northern Europe
Newman, Paul, 1981, Grandeur & Decay (Clevedon Pier)
Newman, Paul, 1976, Channel Passage
North Somerset Council, 2000, The Gordano Round
Pevsner, Nikolaus, 1958, North Somerset and Bristol
Poole, Sharon, 1989, Around Weston-super-Mare in Old Photographs
Quinn, Phil, 1999, The Holy Wells of Bath & Bristol Region
Rippon, Stephen, 1997, The Severn Estuary
Rendell, Stan & Joan, 1997, Banwell through the Ages
Renton, R.S. 1969, Clevedon Parish Church
Rich, John, 1985, Pill in Old Picture Postcards
Rich, John, 1996, The Bristol Pilots
Ryall, Sue, 1999, The People's Village, Memories of Kewstoke
Salmon, Arthur L. 1906, Literary Rambles in the West of England
Savage, R.J.G. 1977, Geological Excursions in the Bristol District
Smith, Graham, 1991, Shipwrecks of the Bristol Channel
Strange, Peter, 1989, The Weston, Clevedon & Portishead Railway
Stuckey, Peter J. 1999, The Sailing Pilots of the Bristol Channel
The National Trust, 1986, Clevedon Court
Thomas, Ethel, 1977, The Avonmouth Story
Tomalin, D.J. & Crook, C.D. 1993, Woodspring Priory
Tozer, Michael, 1989, Around Nailsea, Long Ashton & Yatton in Old Photographs
Waters, Brian, 1955, The Bristol Channel
Wigan, Eve, 1932, Portishead Parish History
Wigan, Eve & Reid A.B.L. 1971 The Tale of Gordano
Williams, Michael, 1998, Portishead
Withers, C.D. 1995, The Story of St. Mary's Walton, Clevedon
Yatton Local History Society, 1991, A History of Yatton
Yatton Local History Society, The 'Yatton Yesterdays' series

We have now endeavoured to lay before our readers, distinctly and forcibly, that which in common estimation
posseses a ray of interest to the stranger of this locality, - and here we must take our leave of him;
but ere doing so, we feign would indulge the hope, that those who have followed us in our peregrinations,
and compared and parallelised our remarks with those charming, delightful, and rural scenes to which they
direct attention, that such have not been altogether disappointed in the execution of our labours; and though
devoid it may be of classic worth, or of literary excellence, yet we hope it does possess some claims, to render
it compatible with its professing purpose: that to some, and perhaps more than some, it may and will prove
a useful vehicle of instruction and information; a truthful guide to this delightful spot, enhancing the interest
of their seaside tarriance, and mantling it with a charm of long remembrance.

The Portishead Guide and Visitor's Hand-book 1855
by Bond & Fardon